The Superschool and the Superstate: American Education in the Twentieth Century, 1918-1970

Studies in the History of American Education Series

Henry J. Perkinson
and Vincent P. Lannie
General Editors

Sheldon Cohen
A History of Colonial Education, 1607–1776
David Madsen
Early National Education, 1776–1830
Frederick M. Binder
The Age of the Common School, 1830–1865
Patricia Albjerg Graham
Community and Class in American Education, 1865–1918
Edgar Gumbert and Joel H. Spring
The Superschool and the Superstate:
American Education in the Twentieth Century, 1918–1970

The Superschool and the Superstate: American Education in the Twentieth Century, 1918-1970

Edgar B. Gumbert
Georgia State University

Joel H. Spring
Case Western Reserve University

John Wiley & Sons, Inc., New York · London · Sydney · Toronto

Library of Congress Cataloging in Publication Data:

Gumbert, Edgar B   1931–
  The superschool and the superstate.

  (Studies in the history of American education series)
  Bibliography: p.
  1. Education—United States—History. I. Spring,
Joel H., joint author. II. Title.

LA210.G85   1974   370′.973   73–22226
ISBN 0–471–33335–2
ISBN 0–471–33336–0 (pbk.)

Printed in the United States of America

10 9 8 7 6 5 4 3 2 1

series preface

This series provides new interpretations of American educational history based on the best recent scholarship. It contains five volumes that present, chronologically and topically, the history of American education from the beginning to the present day.

Each volume gives an original analysis and interpretation of the development of formal and informal agencies of education during a particular period.

Henry J. Perkinson

contents

The Superschool and the Superstate: American Education in the Twentieth Century, 1918-1970

introduction: an interpretive framework

In *The American Mind* Henry Steele Commager located the major turning point in America's development in the nineteenth century. "The decade of the nineties," he wrote, "is the watershed of American history." By 1918 modern America was well along in the making. Science and technology, industrialization and urbanization, corporations and trade unions, bureaucracy and shifts in the class and power structure were the most prominent shaping forces. They at once set the problems to which the nation had to turn and suggested the solutions that it could apply.

The most compelling and persistent problem to emerge from the transformation of society wrought by these forces, the one around which the other problems clustered, was social justice. In Walter Lippman's words, it was "the ancient but ever new problem of liberty and order."

Three major theories informed discussion of the problem of liberty and order. All of them are familiar in Western political and intellectual history, and all of them were put forward for consideration by supporters at various times throughout the twentieth century. Although obviously not entirely adequate, we will use the traditional labels for them. They represent

3

normative models against which events can be juxtaposed.

The conservative model highlights primarily the persisting aspects of society. It stresses the bonds that tie the individual to the group. The just society, according to conservative theory, consists of a social hierarchy of functionally related classes. There is a symbiotic relationship between each class and the whole. The hierarchy is governed by a system of interconnected rights and duties. It is accepted without conflict as long as each class carries out its function properly and contributes to the welfare of the whole. Classes are valued because of what they contribute to the preservation of the hierarchy.

Conservative theory tends to see change as harmful or unnecessary, as a falling away from something better; therefore it tries to obstruct it or to ignore it. The theory holds that a just society is at rest. Dissension or envy between classes disrupts the hierarchical arrangements and leads to change, decay, and injustice.

In conservative theory the free development of the individual is equated with social discipline, with subordination and allegiance to the whole, and with willing acceptance of the class placement. Each member has specific roles and duties to perform, and if properly exercised, the individual contributes both to himself and to society.

Conservative theory claims that individual ability is highly variable. The different statuses and styles of life are outlined by birth and by tradition. That is to say, class position is biologically and historically determined. Ability and class position are perfectly correlated, and it is best not to tamper with them in the schools or in other social institutions. Thus, in the conservative theory order and inequality are linked explicitly.

According to the liberal model, an individual's freedom is based on and protected by legal sanctions. The liberal model is concerned less with the problem of how to integrate the individual with the group than with the deprivation and stunting of the individual on the one hand and with the social arrangements that allow individual freedom and self-realization on the other. The bonds between the individual and the group are not stressed; the emphasis is on the importance of individual liberty and rights. Individualism is held to possess great intellectual and moral resources.

Individual abilities in this model, as in the conservative model, are variable. The liberal model is not against inequality; it is against privilege. The liberal view of society consists of a hierarchy, but theoretically the hierarchy is arrived at from a position of initial equality. Placement in the hierarchy is not by birth or by time-honored tradition; it is by individual attainment.

Liberal theory, then, stresses equality of opportunity. In selective educational institutions, higher ability would always lead to higher rates of admission. Access to education should not, according to this theory, be greater in the more favored classes; ability, not social class position, should determine the distribution of education.

Schooling is seen as an opportunity; the burden of proof is on the individual who, through his own initiative and enterprise, must make use of it. Thus, according to this view, to use Ivan Illich's example, the hereditary inferiority of the serf or the slave is replaced by the inferiority of the school dropout—who is held personally responsible for his failure. Educational circles are obliged to find means to motivate students, a theme discussed *ad nauseum* in endless teacher workshops throughout the twentieth century. Special ability and talent are searched for and encouraged. This leads to a society governed by an aristocracy of talent, to a "meritocracy," as Michael Young called it.

In the late nineteenth century a negative liberalism, as formulated by John Stuart Mill, for example, held that the desired ends could best be achieved with minimum activity on the part of the state. By the beginning of the twentieth century, however, a positive liberalism had developed that held that the state should actively intervene to help regulate the conditions of the race for unequal position.

In both the conservative and liberal models those who stay longer in school earn the right to more wealth, power, and prestige. Those who drop out, or fall out, have to be taught to accept the superiority and special rights, as well as the special duties and obligations, of those who stay. Social position in both theories is comparative; it fosters and depends on feelings of inferiority and superiority. Social stratification is legitimized and rationalized by the schools, particularly in the liberal theory.

The socialist theory of social justice is strictly egalitarian—political, economic, and social. It says that individuals in their original state are equal and that the observable differences that distinguish men result from conventions, particularly from the ways in which their intellect has been employed in the economic system. The end sought by social arrangements in a socialist system is equality of results or equality of condition. A powerful state may or may not be the means by which the end would be achieved. The individual is defined and takes on meaning and significance within a group. Individual development in this theory, as in the conservative theory, depends on group development.

The conservative and socialist models place emphasis on and have strong, carefully worked out theories of community. The liberal theory emphasizes the individual, but has difficulty reconciling its belief in individual fulfillment with a communal ideology. According to liberal theory, the clash of individual egos, competing for their own good, translates itself into a communal good.

In both the conservative and liberal models, "order" means vesting authority in those best able to rule.

Stating the three theories in this way does not adequately indicate their richness, subtlety, or explanatory powers. However, the theories as stated do indicate in broad outline the central points around which social and educational debates took place throughout the twentieth century.

Implied in the above theories is the relationship of education to social mobility. Ralph H. Turner has identified two ideal organizing norms that are useful for analyzing this relationship: sponsored mobility and contest mobility. *"Contest mobility,"* he says, "is a system in which elite status is the prize in an open contest and is taken by the aspirants' own efforts. While the 'contest' is governed by some rules of fair play, the contestants have wide latitude in the strategies they may employ. Since the 'prize' of successful upward mobility is not in the hands of the established elite to give out, the latter are not in a position to determine who shall attain it and who shall not. Under *sponsored* mobility, elite recruits are chosen by the established elite or their agents, and elite status is *given* on the basis of some criterion of supposed merit and cannot be *taken* by any amount of effort or strategy. Upward mobility is like entry into a private club, where each candidate must be 'sponsored' by one or more of the members. Ultimately, the members grant or deny upward mobility on the basis of whether they judge the candidate to have the qualities that they wish to see in fellow members."

It is worth elaborating some of the major distinctions between the two norms as Turner sees them, because they provide a framework for analyzing certain features of American education in the twentieth century.

According to the contest model, elite status can be taken by effort and by meeting criteria that are publicly laid down. Players compete on an equal footing and victory is won by individual efforts. The aim of the system is to give elite membership to those who earn it. Fear of premature judgments is pronounced; selection and a sense of irreparable failure are delayed. Consequently the awarding of elite membership is also delayed. Everybody is encouraged to think of himself as competing for an elite position. Aspirants are not freed from the strains of competitive struggle. The means by which elite credentials are achieved are continuously improved, although disreputable people can still become elite members. A sense of fairness is insisted on. Schooling is presented as an opportunity, and the burden or proof is on the student. Education is valued because of its applicability and practical vocational benefits. Special help is given to some so they can compete better, for example, the Head Start program. The university itself tends to be run like a contest; a series of examinations are set up as hurdles to be overcome. Of course, there is the steady strain from a series of elimination tests.

According to the sponsored model the prize of successful upward mobility is awarded by the established elites. Credentials are presented to them and not to the masses. Recruits are chosen by the elites. There is not much latitude in the strategies that can be employed in upward movement. The criteria of merit are agreed on in advance. Victory goes to the most able, in intellectual terms; the person of moderate intelligence is not expected to be admitted to elite status. A controlled selection procedure is devised; its goal is to make the best use of talents by putting people in their proper place. Belief in the superior competence of the elites is fostered. Recruits are kept under close elite supervision; a norm of paternalism develops. The quality of intellectual activities takes on heightened importance, although in industrial nations the activities tend to be restricted to scientific-technological ones instead of literary-aesthetic ones. Selection for mobility is by intelligence, regardless of social background. Substantial financial aid goes to elite recruits. The chances of a person who does not make the grade in education of moving up by some other means is considerably reduced.

Debates about society and about the means provided for movements within it have been long and persistent. The Declaration of Independence and the Constitution and its Amendments have provided a framework within which important debates have taken place, indeed outside of which some debates are not possible. Although these documents make no explicit reference to education (the Tenth Amendment makes education a responsibility of the states), educational policies can nevertheless be deduced from interpretations of them, as well as being sought elesewhere, for example, in economic organization.

Debates about social mobility and social justice in America have revolved around the issues of liberty and equality and "the general welfare." The connection between them is an old one in Western political and intellectual history. For example, in some eighteenth-century French thought, a rich source of many American ideas, liberty was linked to equality. This tradition was carried on by Marx and has continued to influence educational policy formulations in Russia to the present day.

The trip across the Atlantic almost severed the link between liberty and equality in the United States. Many Americans "love liberty but hate equality." To them equality is opposed to quality of life. On this view the general welfare of the nation can best be advanced and social justice established by noninterference on the part of government. As libertarians see it, the Bill of Rights protects their individual freedom.

However, the link between liberty and equality was not entirely severed by the trip to the United States. There was, and is, the view that social justice is achieved, the general welfare promoted, and individual rights secured when government attempts to provide maximum equality for all. The egalitarian interpretation of the general welfare clause of the Constitution looks to the Declaration of Independence, which makes it possible to link "Life, Liberty and the pursuit of Happiness" to equality.

Throughout the twentieth century conservative thinkers on the whole have supported the libertarian interpretation of the Constitution while liberal thinkers have supported the egalitarian interpretation. But the difference has turned out to be more apparent than real. Both groups of theorists, in contrast to theorists in Europe, supported the contest instead of the sponsored model of social mobility. The differences were only in the rules and conditions of the contest.

Their agreement on the contest model of mobility in turn

led to agreement, seriously challenged only in the 1960s, that the essence of the democratic ethos is in the principle of "equality of opportunity"—an agreement somewhat surprising, given the alleged cultural and ideological pluralism in the United States. Thus liberty and equality came together in the doctrine of equality of opportunity. Conservatives in the United States accepted it because they saw that it, in fact, served the same purposes as the sponsored model; it provided a control mechanism against too much upward mobility. To liberals it seemed to allow individual development.

Conservatism in Western culture historically has had as one of its major objectives the preservation of organic "community." From Plato and Aristotle through the communalism of the Middle Ages to Edmund Burke and G.W.F. Hegel in the nineteenth century and beyond, many thinkers have given the group precedence over the individual, indeed have sought to show that the individual finds meaning and significance only in a group. It has been held by conservative thinkers that community, because of its superior human qualities and its near-mystical values, enhances human existence in a way that society, class, party, or other specific institutions cannot. In 1887 the German sociologist Ferdinand Toennies conceptualized the difference when he distinguished between *gemeinschaft* (community) and *gesellschaft* (society).

This link between conservatism and community was broken, some would say fatally broken, in the United States. Conservative thinkers influenced by the frontier experience, by the Protestant ethic, by evolutionary biological theory, and particularly by private enterprise economic theory in America came to advocate what they liked to call "rugged individualism."

Thinkers operating within the liberal tradition also favored individualism and the satisfaction of individual wants. In this way individualism, independence, and self-assertion fused to become the reigning orthodoxy in the United States by the opening of the twentieth century. Individuals were linked by the structures of society, not by the values and bonds of community.

Individualism, American style, went hand in hand with competition. The economic system, indeed the whole social system, strained toward them as ideal-typical norms. Supporters held that free individuals in open competition were the source of American greatness. The system was kept going by the stick of insecurity and discontent, even of fear and anger, and by the carrot of the rich rewards of money and power for the winners. Aggressiveness, ambition, and desire to top the other fellow were thought to be necessary character traits. Neither future generations nor one's neighbor needed particularly to be taken into account. The renunciation of aggressiveness and competition (which are or can be forms of violence) was thought to endanger society. Many of these views persist.

The consensus attachment to individualism was not without its critics. John Dewey, for example, in writings dating to the late nineteenth century, sought a cohesive community with shared values, needs, and goals *and* the development of the individual. He believed that people could rule themselves without sacrificing either collective welfare or personal freedom.

Edgar Z. Friedenberg in 1970 claimed that it is "the lethal and invidious commitment to individualism that disqualifies Americans for civic responsibility . . . destroying the commune through slovenliness and irresponsibility as surely as it drives the failing executive to suicide."

Also in 1970, in *The Pursuit of Loneliness*, Phillip E. Slater argued that Americans had created and maintained a society that frustrated "the desire for community—the wish to live in trust and fraternal cooperation with one's fellows in a total and visible collective entity." Individualistic striving for the products and power of a technologically driven system were seen as the roots of this frustration.

Related to this issue, Slater argued intriguingly that "the

avoiding tendency lies at the very root of American character. This nation was settled and continuously repopulated by people who were not personally successful in confronting the social conditions obtaining in their mother country, but fled these conditions in the hope of a better life. This series of choices (reproduced in the westward movement) provided a complex selection process—populating America disproportionately with a certain kind of person." Slater argued that "If we gained the energetic and the daring we also gained the lion's share of the rootless, the unscrupulous, those who value money over relationships, and those who put self-aggrandizement ahead of love and loyalty. And most of all, we gained a critically undue proportion of persons who, when faced with a difficult situation, tended to chuck the whole thing and flee to a new environment. Escaping, evading, and avoiding are responses which lie at the base of much that is peculiarly American—the suburb, the automobile, the self-service store and so on."

In an interdependent society, individuals are required to sacrifice for common concerns. The critics above, among many others, argued that Americans in the twentieth century were ideologically and psychologically ill-equipped for the task. The emphasis on individualism made it difficult to get a clear consensus regarding the kind of community they wanted. The culture they created was atomized and diffuse, and was particularly volatile in the cities. It was claimed that Americans were unwilling or unable to share ideals and values sufficiently, and therefore did not carry out public obligations beyond a bare minimum.

It seems incontestable that an unwillingness to spend for public needs was one cause, and probably a major one, of the tragic social decay vividly brought to the nation's attention, particularly by blacks, students, and various minority groups, in the 1960s.

Perhaps alone among technologically advanced nations in the twentieth century, the United States did not have an adequate ideological rationale with which to build a democratic welfare state. If the doctrine of equality of opportunity was appropriate for the early decades of the century—even perhaps for the first half of the century—its adequacy in the context of the "postindustrial" America of the late 1950s and the 1960s was questioned. John McDermott in 1969 claimed that "In technologically advanced societies, equality of opportunity functions as a hierarchical principle, in opposition to the equalitarian social goals it pretends to serve. To the extent that it has already become the kind of 'equality' we seek to institute in our society, it is one of the main factors contributing to the widening gap between the cultures of upper and lower class America." Alternative principles were not widely accepted.

Both major political parties in the United States saw that there were social barriers to the proper application in education of the doctrine of equality of opportunity. They agreed that the federal government should intervene to insure that the necessary social conditions were met. It was accepted that some conditions facilitated and some detracted from educational achievement. Gross inequalities of opportunity caused by race and by social class were singled out for attention. The main difference between the two parties was the speed with which they acknowledged the inequalities and the extent to which they were prepared to use the resources of the government to reduce them. Both parties, however, worked toward a hierarchical society created by a contest.

chapter one

politics, social justice, and the schools

Keeping the contest fair was a political objective throughout the period from 1918 to 1970. This took the form of trying to maintain a tolerable balance among various segments of the population; certain groups were promoted while others were restricted. Essentially four types of legislative actions were used: granting land or cash subsidies to selected groups; enactment of statutes giving special attention to certain groups in order to strengthen them in their competition with others; the creation of investigative and especially regulative agencies to supervise the conduct of selected groups; and laws designed to protect the personal well-being of selected groups.

In the nonpresidential elections of 1910, Theodore Roosevelt came out of retirement to aid Republican candidates for political office. He put forward a program of political, social, and economic reform that he called the "New Nationalism" and the "Square Deal." The federal government, Roosevelt claimed, was obliged to promote social justice and human welfare. "I mean," Roosevelt said, "not merely that I stand for fair play under the present rules of the game but that I stand for having the rules changed so as to work for a more substantial equality of opportunity and of reward for equally good services." The "rule" changes that Roosevelt wanted included, along with others, federal regulation of corporations, income and inheritance taxes, labor codes, and regulations on child labor. Roosevelt's equality of rewards "for equally good services" was intended for both winners and losers. It was not a system designed to eliminate the race or the rewards; it was certainly not intended to assure equality of results.

In the presidential election of 1912 Roosevelt ran on the Progressive or "Bull Moose" party platform. The party platform proposed to safeguard "human resources through an enlightened measure of social and industrial justice." Roosevelt felt that human rights should not be subordinate to property rights; "every man," he said, "holds his property subject to the general right of the community to regulate its use to whatever degree the public welfare may require it."

Roosevelt's proposals were in the Hamiltonian tradition. A powerful central government, he claimed, should be the instrument through which social and economic justice could be achieved, primarily by regulating the activities of big corporations.

Running on the Democratic party ticket in that election, Woodrow Wilson proposed a "New Freedom" in the Jeffersonian tradition. The growth of corporations should be limited, he claimed, small businesses should be encouraged, competition restored and states' rights and powers should be preserved.

Roosevelt held that the government's power should be used in a positive way, to "exalt the lowly and give heart to the humble and downtrodden," as he said. Wilson wanted the federal government to guarantee freedom. By this he meant that federal power should be used to insure fair competition; he did not want to eliminate or reduce competition. In the liberal tradition, he was opposed to privilege, primarily because it reduced enterprise. His "New Freedom" of 1912 sought to use government to create conditions that would allow *laissez faire* to flourish. "Men of business," he claimed, should be free from "the law of legislation and artificial arrangement."

After winning the presidency, his antitrust legislation was in the same tradition. In his special message to Congress in 1914 he said: "What we are purposing to do is . . . not to hamper or interfere with business as enlightened businessmen prefer to do it, or in any sense to put it under ban."

However, the passage in 1914 of the Federal Trade Commission Act and the Clayton Antitrust Act indicated that Wilson was moving toward the principles of government intervention advocated by Roosevelt. By 1916 he largely had abandoned his earlier economic views. Like Roosevelt, he wanted to have the rules of the game changed so government could promote more equality of opportunity; and he sought through his social justice legislation to protect men from the worst ravages of losing in the modified competitive race. With little hesitation after 1916 he undertook to get legislation accepted that had been proposed by liberals and progressives since the turn of the century. As he pointed out, his administration came "very near to carrying out the platform of the Progressive Party."

Under Wilson the Democratic party became capable of implementing national reforms. The lines are clear. The progressive social and economic reforms advanced by Theodore Roosevelt were absorbed by Wilson; they also pointed to a progressivism in the future; the reform legislation of the "Democratic Roosevelt" of the 1930s owed much to the assumptions and proposals of the lapsed "Republican Roosevelt" and the Progressive Party platform of 1912.

During this period and against this background the schools were the objects of serious investigation and public debate. By 1918 all states had passed compulsory education laws. Thereafter secondary education underwent great expansion. Challenged by industrialism, commercialism, and urbanization, the educational system was open to new and pressing demands. A large number of students used the secondary schools for purposes other than preparing for college. Reconsideration of broad educational policy was an urgent necessity.

To undertake this task, the National Education Association

appointed the Commission on the Reorganization of Secondary Education. Its report in 1918, *Cardinal Principles of Secondary Education*, was influenced by political progressivism and by several strands of American educational thought. The influences were society-centered. Traditionally, American schools had been given broad social responsibilities. In the eighteenth century Thomas Jefferson saw schools as the foundations on which democratic institutions could be built. Benjamin Franklin gave to the schools the practical task of preparing young-sters for work. In the nineteenth century Horace Mann sought to use the schools to inculcate the sober moral attitudes necessary for democracy and for commercial advancement. In 1916 in *Democracy and Education* John Dewey proposed the schools as agents of democratic political socialization. These civic-vocational-moral functions were continued by the report of the Commission.

The Commission felt that it would not be possible to educate the masses in the same manner that an intellectual elite formerly had been educated. The seven *Cardinal Principles* stressed the social purposes of education. Preparation for college was less important than it had been. Education for mass consumption, according to the report, included health, command of fundamental processes, worthy home membership, vocation, citizenship, worthy use of leisure time, and ethical character. The "social gospel" of the *Cardinal Principles* influenced subsequent educational thinking, particularly in the 1930s and 1940s, and set the tone for the schools, in part, at least, right up to 1970.

The report accepted collective social democracy. It said, "The purpose of democracy is so to organize society that each member may develop his personality *primarily* through activities designed for the well-being of his fellow members and of society as a whole . . .

"Consequently, education in a democracy, both within and without the school, should develop in each individual the knowledge, interests, ideals, habits and powers whereby he will find his place and use that place to shape both himself and society toward ever nobler ends."

We have added the emphasis. But the authors of the *Cardinal Principles* saw the urgent need, in an industrial and pluralistic society, to try to create community. However, the difficulties of translating the subtleties and the complexities of communitarian democracy into practical educational programs in general were too much to overcome. Stress was given to the more easily understood and the more obviously useful objectives such as health, vocation, and worthy home membership. Citizenship education frequently was a travesty of education for community.

Moreover, a tradition of child-centered pedagogy existed that, while it did not entirely ignore the social roles of education, nevertheless focused attention less on community than on individual development. Early in the century G. Stanley Hall argued that school programs and practices should be based on the natural growth and development of children. Children had particular backgrounds, natures, and needs that had to be taken into account. The school, Hall said, should adjust to the child, not the reverse.

Although he saw the political dimensions of education, John Dewey also held views that supported a type of child-centered education. In 1899 in *The School and Society* he called for an education in which "the child becomes the sun about which the appliances of education revolve." In 1902 in *The Child and the Curriculum* he urged that subject matter in the schools be carefully and "meaningfully" connected to the experiences of children.

The child-centered tradition was strong in the 1920s and was reinforced by the work of the Progressive Education Association, founded in 1919. The PEA represented a break with the society-centered political progressivism. Prominent child-centered educators held the view that "Each child is a law unto himself." Unique and essentially good, the nature of the child, they said, should be the organizing principle of instruction. The focus of teaching should switch from academic subjects to the needs of children. In 1928 in *The Child-Centered School* Harold Rugg and Ann Shumaker advanced the view that creative self-expression instead of deliberate social reform was the appropriate educational response in an urban-industrial civilization. Individual betterment, they believed, ultimately would lead to social improvement.

Although child-centered theory did not always link the schools clearly and directly to larger social purposes, they frequently were linked when the theory was applied. Thus although child-centered theory was advanced by progressive thinkers, it was possible to turn it to conservative ends. For instance, by focusing on individual needs the theory drew attention away from needed social change. Furthermore, the powerful social and economic forces that were opposed to the communal ethos were not averse to a controlled society. The doctrine of individual differences associated with child-centered theory lent itself to this objective, as it provided a rationale for manipulating the vocational destinies of students.

The larger sociopolitical context in the 1920s favored acceptance of many of the tenets of child-centered pedagogy. Progressivism as a political force lost much of its middle-class support and declined as an effective agent of national reconstruction. Although not dead, it lay dormant. Conservative opinion dominated the nation. In the presidential election of 1920, the overwhelming victory of the Republican candidate, Warren G. Harding, over the Democratic nominee, James M. Cox, indicated the desire of Americans to turn away from a world in which conditions, both at home and abroad, were undergoing rapid and relentless change. They wanted to return to simpler, more familiar times. Harding provided the calming, soothing touch that the voters apparently wanted. "America's present need," he said, "is not heroics but healing; not nostrums but normalcy; not revolution but restoration; . . . not surgery but serenity."

Conservative Republicanism dominated the White House

throughout the 1920s, indeed, until Franklin Roosevelt's first term in 1933. Business was not regarded with suspicion; trusts were no longer threatened. Business leaders were held in high esteem. It was believed that government, instead of regulating business, should cooperate with it and assist it in its growth. Aided by the Supreme Court, the federal government followed a "doctrine of business expediency." Herbert Hoover asserted that "The sole function of government is to bring about a condition of affairs favorable to the beneficial development of private enterprise." It was widely assumed that with the growth and development of large corporations there would be larger profits, greater employment, and higher wages; in short, that corporate wealth would somehow inevitably be diffused throughout the populace. If given the necessary incentives, such as tax reductions, and if left alone, business would provide the economic growth and the increase in the standard of living, that is, private consumption, that the nation wanted.

After Harding's death in August, 1923, his successor, Calvin Coolidge, continued to hold forcefully to the principles of individualistic capitalism. Individual enterprise was the prevailing norm; financial success was the dominant objective in life. Coolidge observed that "the attitude of the Chamber of Commerce . . . very accurately reflects that of public opinion generally." Evidently most Americans agreed with Coolidge's statement that "the business of America is business."

Business became a way of life; it was "our American system," as Hoover was fond of saying; "socialism" and "bureaucratic controls" were not. Sinclair Lewis had Babbitt tell his children: "The first thing you got to understand is that all this uplift and flip flop and settlement work and recreation is nothing in God's world but the entering wedge of socialism. The sooner a man learns he isn't going to be coddled, and he needn't expect a lot of free grub . . . the sooner he'll get on the job and produce, produce, produce. That's what this country needs."

It might be thought that the object of this frenzied work

and production was the creation of wealth. But apparently that alone was not a noble enough incentive. "The ultimate result to be desired," Coolidge claimed," is not the making of money, but the making of people. Industry, thrift, and self-control are not sought because they create wealth, but because they create character." In earlier times these traits were believed to create both wealth and character; in the age of the corporation they were devoted to the creation of character alone.

The "American system," then, was designed to produce a nation of virtuous people. The preoccupation with virtue and with character was an American tradition going back to the founding Puritans. Schools from their founding had been enlisted in the service of helping to nourish them. In the 1920s schools were seen as a means of preventing delinquency. Attention to virtue and to character in the 1920s was perhaps particularly well placed. Disillusionment with the war and with the postwar world created a mental state conducive to political insecurity and to intolerance. Blinkered patriotism, conformity in intellectual matters, fear of a vaguely conceived "radicalism" and hostility toward things unconventional, alien, or "un-American" sprang up, and they have proven to be persistent qualities.

Moreover, the pervasiveness of the business ethic was not without dangers. The "hot air" culture was developed enthusiastically in the Twenties. Advertising, promotion, and successful salesmanship, including "selling oneself," emerged as an acceptable life-style. The schools, once again, were enlisted in the campaign of forming the characteristics necessary for "getting ahead." They helped to integrate youth into the emerging corporate society.

Some unsavory characteristics developed and were rewarded. Egotism, aggressiveness, lack of scruple, disrespect for law (the Eighteenth Amendment making Prohibition the law of the land was passed in 1919 and was widely broken thereafter), and "boosterism," a simplicity bordering on self-deception, were among the qualities that took root and flourished. Several are thought by observers, Americans and foreigners alike, to be lasting characteristics in American life.

Unprecedented business growth characterized the 1920s. Giant corporations dominated the economic system. From 1922 to 1929 the average profit of the leading manufacturing corporations was over 11 percent a year. Production in all branches of the economy increased by 46 percent between 1920 and 1929. New industries were developed, such as those producing automobiles, airplanes, chemicals, and electric power. Motion pictures and radio were started. Both had great potential for molding public opinion and were important parts of the informal educational system. Their relationship to the formal educational system has remained constant; formal education is a public responsibility, while informal education has remained largely under private control.

Throughout the 1920s there were shifts in the labor force. In general the number of workers in professional, service, and clerical occupations increased. Because of new invention, new sources of power and increased labor efficiency, the numbers of workers in factories, mining, and transportation decreased. In 1920 65 percent of the employed population was engaged directly in production; in 1930 the figure was 56 percent. The productive labor of youth in particular was less in demand. Agriculture was rapidly mechanized, and this caused a decline in the number of farmers and farm laborers. The movement from country to city continued with only a small setback during the Depression of the 1930s.

Despite the many changes in society an uncritical economic optimism prevailed. Business leadership went unchallenged. In the presidential election of 1928 Hoover and the Republican party were the spokesmen for big business. But the Democratic party under the leadership of its nominee, Alfred E. Smith, did not wish to challenge these interests either. After his election in 1928, Hoover declared his war on poverty. "We in America today are nearer to the final triumph over poverty than ever before in the history of any land. The poorhouse is vanishing from among us. We have not reached the goal, but given a chance to go forward with the policies of the last eight years, we shall soon, with the help of God, be in sight of the day when poverty will be banished from this nation. There is no guaranty against poverty equal to a job for every man. That is the primary purpose of the policies we advocate."

Behind Hoover's optimistic talk were real grievances. Poverty did in fact exist; indeed, in 1929 60 percent of all families had incomes below $2000, which the Brookings Institution considered to be the poverty line. Inequality in income and status increased despite the increased earnings of corporations. Although wage earners received larger incomes, their share of the total national income dropped; the largest gains were made by salaried executives and by stockholders.

Moreover, the workers whose jobs were threatened or eliminated by the industrial changes did not share Hoover's sanguinity, although their plight was largely overlooked until after the economic collapse in 1929. Skilled workers declined in importance, because in the new mechanized industries semiskilled workers were more sought after. Some employers adopted certain features of welfare capitalism—safety devices, recreation facilities, and improved sanitation—and this reduced labor militancy. The courts frequently granted injunctions limiting the power of the unions; employers campaigned for open shops or operated company unions. The American Federation of Labor, composed of privileged workers, conservatively protected its few gains and desisted on the whole from recruiting either Negroes or unskilled workers. Total union membership decreased from 5.1 million in 1920 to 4.3 million in 1929. The number of unemployed fluctuated; estimates put the figure at never less than 2 million, and at more than that figure in 1922 and 1924.

The great Wall Street Crash in October 1929 plunged the nation into financial panic. For the next 2½ years the stock market coasted slowly downward. It was the start of the Great

Depression, from which relief did not come until the growth of war industries in the 1940s. During the 1920s the conventional wisdom was that the public automatically was served if business interests were furthered. This view prevailed even after the stock market crash. When Hoover put his proposals for ending the Depression into effect, they were based on the assumption that the economy would recover if the business community could be helped. Instead of distributing money to unemployed workers and other destitute people at the bottom of the economic system, Hoover gave financial aid to business institutions at the top of the system. The Reconstruction Finance Corporation, for example, was established to lend money to banks, insurance companies, building and loan associations, and other like institutions needing aid. New York Congressman Fiorello La Guardia called it "the millionaire's dole." Hoover did, however, arrange for federal funds to be loaned to states requiring capital. To aid individual property owners, he set up the Home Owners' Loan Corporation to prevent mortgage foreclosures.

Nevertheless, the nation continued in the worst depression it ever had encountered. Unemployment, business ruin, and actual hunger faced many people. Since the end of World War I, Americans had deferred to entrepreneurial business leaders, but with the onset of the Depression these leaders did not seem to know what to do. In the presidential election of 1932 the Republican party nominated Hoover for a second term. The Democratic party nominated and elected the governor of New York, Franklin Delano Roosevelt, and also established large Democratic majorities in Congress.

In March 1933 Roosevelt took over the difficult task of trying to lead the country out of economic chaos. American capitalism was in a critical situation. The cluster of values associated with it—"rugged individualism," heavy reliance on monetary incentives and rewards, and the achievement ethic—were challenged. Left-wing social movements and intellectual radicalism were revived. Fear, desperation, pessimism, and doubts about democratic processes were prevalent.

The election of Roosevelt marked the recognition that the United States had become an interdependent industrial economy. The Depression so impressed enough Americans that they were prepared to alter some of their social, political, and economic ideas and practices. They sought to construct, or reconstruct, a corporate social life. Anne O'Hare McCormick hoped that the election of 1932 might help to turn "... sentimental, agitated but uninformed Americanism into positive and adventurous citizenship."

The public schools, of course, were not unaffected by the Depression. At the simplest and most obvious level pressures to reduce educational expenditures developed. There were reductions in school revenues and in many schools activities were curtailed. Tuition was charged in some communities, schools were closed in others.

At another level, the framework of economic collapse, ideological confusion, and political experimentation within which the schools operated stimulated educators to reconsider the purposes of education and the role the schools might play in the troubled times.

The Depression switched attention of some educators who had been interested in it in the 1920s from child-centered education to social reconstructionism. Social engineering was widely discussed. Teachers College, Columbia University, was the center in which John Dewey, William H. Kilpatrick, George S. Counts, John L. Childs, and other social reconstructionists formulated the educational policies they thought appropriate for the conditions of the 1930s. In 1933 they published *The Educational Frontier*, edited by Kilpatrick. In it they claimed that education was "to prepare individuals to take part intelligently in the management of conditions under which they live, to bring them to an understanding of the forces which are moving, (and) to equip them with the intellectual and practical tools by which they can themselves enter into direction of these forces."

In 1934 the first issue of the progressive journal, *The Social Frontier*, claimed that *laissez faire* individualism was at an end, that it had been replaced by economic and social planning for social welfare. It directed its attention to "those formative influences and agencies which serve to induct the individual —whether old or young—into the life and culture of the group . . . it address(es) itself to the task of considering the broad role of education in advancing the welfare and interests of the great masses of the people who do the work of society . . ."

In the same year the Commission on the Social Studies in the Schools appointed by the American Historical Association published its final recommendations on instruction in the schools. The report supported the social reconstructionists' position. It declared that "the age of individualism and *laissez faire* in economy and government is closing and that a new age of collectivism is emerging." It said that "If education continues to emphasize the philosophy of individualism in economy, it will increase the accompanying social tensions." In a "closely integrated society," it said, the schools should actively support reform toward a socialized society.

The social reconstructionists advocated switching the focus of the schools from academic subjects to social and community needs and problems. Following Dewey, they held that the school had a role to play in reforming and humanizing industrial civilization. Although they were ambiguous about how far the teacher should go toward indoctrination, all agreed that teachers could help bring about political reform. The school, they said, should be a place where cooperation and self-government could be learned and practiced. While the schools alone could not change industrial civilization, in cooperation with other groups they could assist in rejuvenating it.

These reports and journals had little influence on either school practice or policy. Schoolmen were concerned less with the abstractions of collectivism than with more specific and immediate pedagogical issues.

Moreover, the Democratic party platform for the election

of 1932 was basically a conservative document. Among other things it promised a 25 percent reduction in government expenditures, a balanced budget, and no government interference with private enterprise. The years 1933 and 1934 saw no radical legislation and no major changes in the structure of the economy. Much of the legislation passed was quite acceptable to business interests. The National Industrial Recovery Act, for example, had its origins in activities of the Chamber of Commerce and of trade associations started by businessmen in the 1920s to set standards and to restrict competition. Roosevelt sought to bring business groups into his programs and he saw the N.I.R.A. as a sign of industry-labor cooperation that could head off the need for more radical legislation.

The need to bring about economic recovery dominated the early months of Roosevelt's "New Deal." Roosevelt said in his campaign for election in 1932 that the main task to be undertaken was not the expansion of business but the solution of the problem of underconsumption. The solution of this problem turned on solving the problem of unemployment. In 1933 unemployment reached an estimated 25 percent of the labor force; it never dropped below 14 percent for the entire decade. In the winter of 1935 to 1936 unemployment was over 10 million; in June 1936 it was down to 6 million; in August 1937 it had dropped to under 5 million; but by May 1938 it had increased to a little over 9½ million. Unemployment came to be regarded by Roosevelt and the New Deal as a misfortune caused by conditions beyond his control instead of as a fault of the unemployed worker.

As governor of New York, Roosevelt had said "aid must be extended by Government, not as a matter of charity, but as a matter of social duty." This principle served as a guideline when he was president. In a speech during the campaign of 1932, he claimed that "Every man has a right to life; and this means that he has also a right to make a comfortable living . . ."

Prior to Roosevelt's presidency, government in the main had been restricted to a regulatory role. Roosevelt gave to it enlarged responsibilities. He adopted the view that the state could be expected to help correct social inequalities by appropriate public action. In the 1930s John Maynard Keynes wrote that the "failure to provide for full employment" and the "arbitrary and inequitable distribution of wealth and income" were the main economic problems of the times. The Keynesian idea that the solution of these problems required massive government spending and unbalanced budgets to make up for the decline in private spending was accepted and acted on within limits during the Roosevelt years. To Keynes, and also to Roosevelt, the government should become involved actively in the distribution of wealth so as to benefit certain deprived groups and classes.

Inequality was a central and persistent theme throughout the 1930s; it was dropped as a major issue only after World War II. In his State of the Union message of January 1935, Roosevelt declared: "We find our population suffering from old inequalities, little changed by past sporadic remedies. In spite of our efforts and in spite of our talk, we have not weeded out the over-privileged, and we have not effectively lifted up the underprivileged. . . . We do not destroy ambition, nor do we seek to divide our wealth into equal shares on stated occasions. We continue to recognize the greater ability of some to earn more than others. But we do assert that the ambition of the individual to obtain for him and his a proper security, a reasonable leisure, and a decent living throughout life is an ambition to be preferred to the appetite for great wealth and great power."

In the summer of 1935 Congress passed legislation that was designed to help those groups that had benefited least from earlier legislation—the aged, the small farmer, and the small businessman.

In his inaugural address on January 20, 1937, Roosevelt in a famous passage indicated the work that still had to be done by his administration. "In this nation," he said, "I see tens of millions of its citizens—a substantial part of its whole population—who at this very moment are denied the greater part of what the very lowest standards of today call the necessities of life. I see millions of families trying to live on incomes so meager that the pall of family disaster hangs over them day by day. . . . I see millions denied education, recreation, and the opportunity to better their lot and the lot of their children. . . I see one-third of a nation ill-housed, ill-clad, ill-nourished."

Taken together, one result of New Deal legislation was that the balance of power among important groups changed. The New Deal aided groups that formerly had not received much help from the federal government. Although many employers through extensive campaigns tried to give the impression that labor leaders were agitators with Communist leanings, Roosevelt's administration was sympathetic to the unions and took them into partnership. Farmers also gained in importance and power. Lower economic groups became politically more confident and hopeful.

It is true that class antagonisms became more articulate and that social tensions heightened. Roosevelt's rhetoric, if nothing more, would have contributed to this. For example, in his Annual Message to Congress in January 1936, Roosevelt claimed that the enemy was the "minority in business and industry," the "unscrupulous money changers" who stole "the livery of great national constitutional ideals to serve discredited special interests." Nevertheless, class war was not a characteristic of Roosevelt's administration. The New Deal did not weaken one class at the expense of another. Traditional economic privilege and power continued. The largest corporations, with a few exceptions, continued to earn profits.

The traditional political order did not go unchallenged. By 1935 and 1936 political conflict had intensified. There was talk about the "crisis of capitalism." Criticism of Roosevelt's New Deal mounted from both left and right. In 1935 Floyd B.

Olson, Farmer-Labor governor of Minnesota, spoke of the need of a third party to "preach the gospel of government and collective ownership of the means of production." However, New Deal measures had weakened the appeal of left-wing parties. The voting strength of the Socialist party under the leadership of Norman Thomas was smaller in the elections of 1932 and 1936 than it had been in 1920. Although its membership increased from 7545 in 1930 to 25,000 in 1934, the Communist party was not a significant political force.

Insecurity, fear, and humiliation strengthened other movements. Father Charles E. Coughlin called for nationalization of banking and national resources. Dr. Francis E. Townsend put forward a plan for generous old-age pensions. Senator Huey Long of Louisiana began putting together a third-party movement with his Share Our Wealth plan as its vision and organizing principle. It was not without influence. Long's biographer, T. Harry Williams, argues that Roosevelt's tax message of 1935, which observers claim signaled his turn to the left, was made primarily because of the political threat posed by Long and his movement. Nevertheless, the two-party system remained intact.

While the pressures from the left thought that Roosevelt was doing too little for the underprivileged, those from the right felt that he was interfering too much with private enterprise. Big capitalists and small entrepreneurs alike resented New Deal policies. They denounced what they called the New Deal's "tyranny," its "socialistic experiments," and Roosevelt's "unconstitutional dictatorship."

One of the bitterest opponents of the New Deal was the Liberty League, founded in 1934. Financed primarily by Du Pont and General Motors interests, it was an "educational organization" set up to counter the "communistic elements [that] lead the people to believe that all businessmen are crooks."Along with the United States Chamber of Commerce, it pressed for more individual and corporate freedom.

The Liberty League asserted that the lawyers, professors, and labor leaders who helped formulate and support New Deal programs were either Communists or had Communist "leanings." In the campaign for the presidential election of 1936 it was further asserted that many university professors were propagandists for "alien ideologies."

In that election Roosevelt explicitly repudiated attachment to any such ideology. He saw, however, what many conservatives fail to see: that things have to change in order to remain the same. "...the true conservative," Roosevelt said, "is the man who has a real concern for injustice and takes thought against the day of reckoning. The true conservative seeks to protect the system of private property and free enterprise by correcting such injustices and inequalities as arise from it. The most serious threat to our institutions comes from those who refuse to face the need for change. Liberalism becomes the protection of the far-sighted conservative."

Roosevelt was an enlightened conservative. He helped carry out controlled conservative reform from the top in order to prevent uncontrolled radical reform from the bottom. He sought to conserve institutions by gradually adapting them to change. Business was not hurt by the New Deal; if anything, it was given renewed vitality. Roosevelt's aim, he said, was to preserve and strengthen the capitalist system. This he did by palliating the worst effects of the Depression and by humanizing capitalism. Although readier for social reform than the Republican party, nothing the Democratic party did under the leadership of Roosevelt went beyond the capitalist system. Generally the Republicans represented the interests of the big property owners while the Democrats represented those of the small owners. But both were devoted to private property and to the profit system.

Political parties in the United States thus far in the twentieth century have not been cohesive organizations with fixed principles. The Democrats under Roosevelt in the 1930s were no exception. Some critics viewed the New Deal as a threat to the American social, political, and economic system, as a violation of democracy. Others saw it as an unprecedented and enlightened social revolution. Both overstate the case. Instead, the dominant feature of the period was the continuity instead of discontinuity with the American past. An optimist—and opportunist—Roosevelt basically was nonideological. He had no coherent program or overarching philosophy. Huey Long colorfully characterized the disorder of the programs of the New Deal. "What is it? Is it government? Maybe so. It looks more like St. Vitus dance."

Roosevelt moved with majority opinion; his programs grew pragmatically out of the conditions of the times. He had no intention of dramatically departing from or altering the established order. Accommodation, adaptation, adjustment, and evolution were the characteristics of his presidency. Many of the principles of his administration had been applied or accepted before 1933.

Thus, the reforms of the New Deal posed no threat to the fundamental structure of the society. Roosevelt wanted to establish "a democracy of opportunity" based on competition and private property. Contest and hierarchy remained.

Under these conditions schoolmen were not always either clear or in agreement about the relative weight to give to the individual or the group, liberty or equality. In 1932 a committee of the National Education Association formulated 10 "Socio-Economic Goals of America," which also served as general goals of education. It is surprising that in the early years of the Depression no goal explicitly mentioned community; social welfare was mentioned only as a qualifier of the ninth goal, "Freedom." The tenth goal was still the standard interpretation of democratic education—"Fair play and equality of opportunity." The detailed description of the 10 goals invariably went in an individualistic direction.

In 1938 the Educational Policies Commission of the National Education Association continued some aspects of the "social gospel" of the *Cardinal Principles*. Its report, *The Purposes of Education in American Democracy*, referred a few times to what in a loose and general way could be called group values: for example, "puts human relationships first"; "can work with others"; "appreciates the social value of his work"; "is sensitive to the disparities of human circumstances"; "is a cooperating member of a world community"; "accepts his civic duties"; and "acts upon an unswerving loyalty to democratic ideals." But the tenor of the report made it clear that the "democratic ideals" were seen largely in individualistic terms.

Two years later, in 1940, the Educational Policies Commission in some ways seemed to be coming around to the collectivist emphasis of the social reconstructionist educators in the early 1930s. According to the "Hallmarks of Democratic Education" of its publication, *Learning the Ways of Democracy*, "Democratic education has as its central purpose the welfare of all the people." Another "Hallmark" stated that "Democratic education guarantees to all the members of its community the right to share in determining the purposes and policies of education." Still a third "Hallmark" asserted that "Democratic education teaches through experience that every privilege entails a corresponding duty, every authority a responsibility, every responsibility an accounting to the group which granted the privilege or authority."

However, if three of the "Hallmarks" can be interpreted in a collectivist way, the other nine were primarily individualistic. For example, reflecting the liberal tradition so dominant in the 1930s, one "Hallmark" stated that "Democratic education serves each individual with justice, seeking to provide equal educational opportunity for all, regardless of intelligence, race, religion, social status, economic condition, or vocational plans." In the same tradition, another "Hallmark" stated that "Democratic education is concerned for the maintenance of those economic, political, and social conditions which are necessary for the enjoyment of liberty." Liberty and individualism took precedence over equality and community.

In 1944, near the end of World War II, the Educational Policies Commission in another report, *Education for All American*

Youth, continued its confusions and ambiguities pertaining to individualism and community. Already it had pulled back from its few mild references to welfare in the 1940 report. Of its 10 "imperative needs," only two had to do with collective behavior. "All youth," the report said, "need to develop respect for other persons, to grow in their insight into ethical values and principles, and to be able to live and work cooperatively with others." But perhaps the best expression of the ambiguities surrounding the individual-society issue, and one repeated for decades in hundreds and probably thousands of schools across the country, was the statement that "All youth need to understand the rights and duties of the citizen of a democratic society, and to be diligent and competent in the performance of their obligations as members of the community and citizens of the state and nation." Production and consumption of goods received as much—and clearer—emphasis.

Roosevelt died suddenly on April 12, 1945 and Vice President Harry S. Truman succeeded to the presidency. In an address in September 1945, Truman said he intended to extend "the progressive and humane principles of the New Deal." Inequality remained an issue to Truman. He held that the federal government existed "not for the benefit of a privileged few, but for the welfare of all the people." For example, in the declaration of purpose of the Employment Act of 1946, Truman managed to have adopted the principle that "it is the continuing policy and responsibility of the Federal Government to use all practicable means ... to promote maximum employment, production and purchasing power." The rhetoric of trouncing big business, popular throughout the 1930s, also remained. In an "antibusiness" speech at Dexter, Iowa, a few weeks before his election in 1948, Truman asserted, "The Wall Street reactionaries are not satisfied with being rich ... they are gluttons of privilege ... Cold men ... cunning men. ... They want a return of the Wall Street dictatorship."

In the New Deal tradition, Truman proposed federal aid to education and national health insurance. Both proposals were defeated. Conservative interests saw them as unwarranted extensions of government power, as "interference" or "meddling," as examples of "creeping socialism." Roman Catholic interests rejected the proposed federal aid to education because it excluded aid to parochial schools. Racists rejected it because they were afraid that federal aid would increase federal control in education and jeopardize local segregated arrangements. The American Medical Association lined up solidly and vigorously against what it liked to call "socialized medicine."

Although the Fair Deal, as Truman called his program, perpetuated the reform tradition, few of his proposals became law. Circumstances had changed political and economic priorities.

Throughout the 1930s the nation had debated seriously the assertion in the Declaration of Independence that "all men are created equal." As before in American history, the debates about equality and justice referred to specific instances of inequality and injustice exhibited in particular circumstances. The demand for equality had come in stages. With the extension of the franchise to women in 1920, political equality for citizens over twenty-one years of age legally had been achieved.

But while political equality was perhaps a necessary condition for achieving other equalities, it alone was not sufficient. It was clear that neither economic nor social nor educational equality followed automatically from political equality. They are not the same thing and, to the extent that they have been attained, they have come at different times. In the 1930s economic equality was given priority, although its meaning was restricted, as we have seen, to equality of opportunity, to the equal right to a job. There were not very strong pressures in the 1930s for equality of consumption or for social equality.

World War II dampened but did not eliminate pressures for equality. The grossest and cruelest inequality remained—that between blacks and whites. In the 1930s a few political and economic rights were quietly extended to Negroes. Although they did not receive their full political and economic rights as guaranteed by the Constitution, their social rights were even more baldly denied.

On May 17, 1954 in *Brown* v. *Board of Education of Topeka* the Supreme Court unanimously ruled that "separate educational facilities are inherently unequal" and that they violated the Fourteenth Amendment's guarantee of "equal protection of the law." A year later, in May 1955, states were required to begin desegration "with all deliberate speed." The most affected states promised "massive resistance" by "all lawful means."

While not perhaps "massive," the resistance continued in 1970. Educational (and, in this case, legal) equality was interpreted, rightly, to be linked in a significant way to social equality: both have to do with consumption, that is, with status. Social equality was extended, theoretically, before anything resembling economic equality had been achieved. The Supreme Court decision meant that in many cases poor blacks were integrated in schools with middle-class whites. What was basically an economic and class problem thus was made to look like a race problem, and in the period since 1955, this deterred the passage of legislation aimed at reducing class differences. If anything, the race conflict blurred the fundamental class differences, which in 1970 were still pronounced, and made the solution to the class problem more difficult.

What we have called the equality issue was really an equality of opportunity issue. The Supreme Court decision on the issue of "separate but equal" schools for Negroes was the end of a long line of equality legislation bringing the different kinds of equality under one covering principle—equality of opportunity. Although passed, the larger normative and institutional context influenced implementation of the equality of opportunity legislation.

After World War II production and economic expansion largely replaced poverty and social justice as the main issues of national debate. As a result of war production, employment was at a high level and there was plenty of money available to spend. Impatient with wartime restrictions, powerful business and industrial interests in their public rhetoric sought to have the government once again foster and promote free competitive enterprise. The National Association of Manufacturers, for example, urged the elimination of government planning and controls. It argued that the reconversion of the economy could best be expedited if the government would "get out of business." Once this was done, the argument went, production would increase rapidly; with increased production the amount of national wealth going to the poor would take care of itself. Tired of the rigors, sacrifices, and inconveniences of the war, the public apparently agreed. The post-World War II view that if business prospered the rest of the nation would automatically prosper was merely a variant on the conventional wisdom of the 1920s. And, as in the 1920s, the voters turned to a Republican administration.

By 1952 the alleged "mess in Washington" dominated the presidential campaign. Hammering away at three issues—Korea, communism, and corruption—the Republican party elected Dwight D. Eisenhower president, the first Republican to hold the White House in 20 years. He was reelected in 1956.

In his inaugural address, Eisenhower proclaimed three goals of his administration—peace, prosperity, and progress. He said he would seek to achieve these goals by traditional conservative policies—lower taxes, economy, reduced government spending, balanced budget, and fiscal obstacles to inflation. The Eisenhower years—from January 1953 to January 1961—on the whole were conformist and complacent, dominated by the hates and the fears of the Cold War. The problems of medical care and of the "crisis in education," as in the late 1940s, were two of the most important problems, but the Eisenhower administration failed to solve them. Like Truman, Eisenhower proposed federal aid to education to help solve the problem of the shortage of teachers and of classrooms; but, as in the Truman administration, a coalition of religious and racist interests successfully prevented the proposed legislation from getting through Congress.

The alleged crisis in education involved more than classrooms and teachers. There always had been critics of public education, and throughout the 1930s and 1940s there had been criticism of the broad social roles that had been given to the schools. In the 1950s both the child-centered and the society-centered approaches of progressive education came under heavy criticism. Critics such as Arthur Bestor and Albert Lynd claimed that progressive education overpsychologized instruction, that it was too indulgent with the pupils, that it was sentimental, and that it did not foster intellectual excellence. Throughout the 1950s and 1960s the assertion that "the gifted students are neglected" was widely heard. Critics also wanted a return to "fundamentals," to a subject-centered education.

On the whole pressures throughout the 1950s to return to a more selective education and to a curriculum organized on the basis of academic disciplines were too strong to resist. Representative of the trend was the report in 1954 of the New York Regents' Council on Readjustment of High School Education, *The Schools We Need—Now and For Tomorrow*. It called for "a stronger emphasis on the three R's and other basic skills" and for "giving gifted children challenges and opportunities equal to their abilities." The differentiating functions instead of the unifying functions of education were stressed, and to aid these functions adequate guidance services were recommended. Vocational education and work experience, when appropriate, were advocated for students who apparently were less than gifted. Special education for girls was suggested. Apart from a passing reference to the work needs of the community and a plea to develop in each youth awareness of his "privileges and responsibilities as an American citizen," group goals were not mentioned. The trend to abandon the mild social collectivism of the 1930s was continued.

The launching of the Russian Sputnik in 1957 strengthened the hand of critics of progressive education, although paradoxically some critics gave the schools even more fateful social functions. The rigid attitudes of the Cold War made it easier for them to translate conflict with Russia into an educational problem. Military preparedness, including skills and attitudes, became a concern of the schools. National survival was at stake, it was claimed. Emphasis was placed on manpower needs, particularly on the need to give greater attention to gifted children. Admiral Hyman Rickover continued this argument into the 1960s.

Manpower needs and military preparedness arguments were used successfully to justify federal aid to education in 1958 in the form of the National Defense Education Act, a comprehensive piece of post-Sputnik crisis legislation. Its approach to the school curriculum was based on academic disciplines. The original act strengthened science, mathematics, and foreign languages; in 1964 it was amended to include English, reading, history, and geography. Among other things it aided students in higher education through loans and fellowships. Vocational educational programs were stimulated. Counseling and guidance services were strengthened in order to aid the schools in their sorting functions.

James B. Conant continued the trend to a more "sponsored" educational program with the publication in 1959 of *The American High School Today*. He argued that highly gifted youngsters were not being sufficiently challenged. Although he rejected the policy of having "tracks," he supported ability grouping in required courses. He called for individualized programs and for special arrangements for academically talented students. Nonacademic vocational and commercial programs were proposed, along with an adequate guidance service to help the schools to channel the students. Equality of opportunity, he held, could best be assured in a comprehensive, multipurpose school instead of in separate institutions, which had been the case traditionally in Europe.

The trend in education evident throughout the 1950s toward elitism and differentiation was capped in 1960 by the White House Conference on Children and Youth. It talked, as progressives had talked, of individual differences and of diversified programs "to meet the needs of all youths." But like the conservative critics of the 1950s it called for special provisions "for both the talented and slow-learning students," and like the critics it saw the need for counseling and guidance services to help put youngsters in their appropriate academic and social places. Community was mentioned in passing.

The critics of the 1950s who reacted against the tenets of progressivism managed to reinstate many educational practices more consistent with libertarian, individualistic democracy and with a stratified, elitist society than with an egalitarian, communal social democracy.

Aid came from an unlikely source. If Teachers College, Columbia University, had been the center of collectivist thinking about education in the 1930s, in the 1950s it had become a seat of libertarian thought. In 1955, the report of the Teachers College Citizenship Education Project, "Improving Citizenship Education," gave heavy stress to freedom and to individualism. The major headings of the report were the free individual, the free government, the free economy, and the free world. A free society was not used as an organizing category, let alone a free community. There were few references to society, community, or social welfare, and they were scattered among the four categories where they drew little attention to themselves. Privileges and responsibilities of corporate enterprise and organized labor were mentioned. Subheadings such as "the rights of property," "the privileges of individual enterprise," and "the privileges of individual labor" accurately indicate the tone of the report.

By the mid-1950s the tensions between the poles of liberty-equality and individual-community had been resolved in both cases in favor of the former. In the 1960s groups fought, against odds, for the nation to turn toward the latter. Egalitarian socialist-style community typically was favored over hierarchical conservative community.

The 1960s opened with a focus in the schools on intellectual processes. In 1961 the Educational Policies Commission in its report, *The Central Purpose of American Education*, asserted that "The purpose which runs through and strengthens all other educational purposes—the common thread of education

—is the development of the ability to think. This is the central purpose to which the school must be oriented if it is to accomplish either its traditional tasks or those newly accentuated by recent changes in the world. To say it is central is not to say that it is the sole purpose or in all circumstances the most important purpose, but that it must be a pervasive concern in the work of the school." The curriculum work in the 1960s of Jerome Bruner, Joseph Schwab, and Edwin Fenton, for example, reflected the renewed cognitive emphasis. Although this educational emphasis sometimes was taken in an egalitarian direction, as in the work of Bruner, the social context lent itself more to an elitist interpretation and application.

By 1960, peace, prosperity, and progress, the three goals Eisenhower had proclaimed in his inaugural address, seemed as far from realization as in 1953. Preoccupied with the Cold War, with the defense of the "Free World," with staying ahead of Russia, and with stopping Communist aggression, the nation during most of the postwar era was in "a rage to achieve," to use Joseph Kraft's vivid phrase. It turned its back on those who did not keep up; it did not look back until violence forced it to, and then only reluctantly. According to Kraft, "Woe unto those who do not participate. If they cannot keep up with the national pace, they are cut off from education, decent housing, good jobs, and even equitable treatment." Preoccupied with the problems of production and economic growth, little attention was paid to the problems of distribution, particularly to the problem of the amount of national wealth going to the poor. It was assumed that because the total national wealth was increasing, everybody was getting richer and generally improving his standard of living. In fact, distribution of income was almost constant throughout the postwar period. In 1947 the poorest fifth of the population received 3.5 percent of total national income; in 1966 it received 3.7 percent. In 1947 the richest fifth received 43.8 percent of the total; in 1966 it received 45.8 percent. As Michael Harrington pointed out in 1962 in *The Other America: Poverty in the United States*, nearly one third of the nation was still "ill-housed, ill-clad, ill-nourished."

If anything, the problem was getting worse. There were significant changes in the occupational structure. In general, the biggest gains were in tertiary production, that is to say in government, the professions, service, and clerical employment. Access to the new jobs required credentials that could be acquired only by attendance in formal and supervised educational and training programs. Because many people lacked these credentials, or were blocked by discrimination from getting them, they were unable to move freely into the work force and, therefore, were locked into their low positions. In the 1960s there were vacant jobs beside unemployed men and women who were unqualified to fill them.

Thus, there was disequilibrium between economic development on the one hand and social justice on the other. Abundance and poverty existed together. Formerly in America the victims of inequities in general had accepted their fate docilely. For example, in the Depression in the 1930s respect for law, order and the rights of property continued unaltered. This changed in the 1960s. The promise of America conflicted too much with the reality. The inequalities became intolerable, and they were a major course of the chronic social strife, the random violence, the drug addiction, and the rising crime rates that faced the nation in that sad decade. The tragic inequalities gave way to an equally tragic disorder. Liberty and order, as Lippman pointed out, long had been identified as related issues in American thought. Liberty and equality long had been seen by many (but not all) as being opposed to each other. In the 1960s equality and order became inextricably linked.

Caught in massive and rapid economic growth during the postwar years, the nation had not bothered to look too closely at the problem of inequality. ("If you stop running you'll fall down.") When it did, it comforted itself with the nearly unanimously held folk norm—the principle of equality of opportunity. This principle had been extended to blacks by the Supreme Court in 1954 during a Republican administration. It was left to Democratic administrations to try to apply the principle throughout most of the 1960s.

In the presidential election of 1960, Democratic nominee John F. Kennedy won a narrow victory over the Republican candidate, Richard M. Nixon. After Kennedy's assassination in November 1963, Vice President Lyndon B. Johnson assumed the presidency. Johnson was elected president in 1964.

Kennedy strived to "get America moving again." He wanted the nation, after several years of privatization, to consider once again problems of the general welfare. The quality of life was an issue. Poverty, inequality, and social injustice were the domestic problems toward which Kennedy's New Frontier and Johnson's Great Society turned. Throughout the 1950s, the "gospel of growth," while it had dominated policy makers, had not gone unexamined. In 1958 John Kenneth Galbraith published *The Affluent Society*, one of the most discussed social critiques of the decade. In it he made a plea for more attention to the public sector—to housing, police, mass transit, education, and welfare. It was a restatement of some observations made by John Maynard Keynes in the 1930s. Keynes held, presciently, that, "When the accumulation of wealth is no longer of high social importance, there will be great changes in the code of morals. We shall be able to rid ourselves of many of the pseudo-moral principles which have hog-ridden us for two hundred years by which we have exalted some of the most distasteful of human qualities into the position of the highest values. We shall be able to afford to dare to assess the money-motive at its true value. . . . All kinds of social customs and economic practices affecting the distribution of wealth which we now maintain at all costs, however distasteful and unjust they may be in themselves . . . we shall then be free, at last, to discard." As Galbraith put it: "I am not quite sure what the advantage is in having a few more dollars to spend if the air is too dirty to breathe, the water too polluted to drink, the streets are filthy and the schools so bad that the young, perhaps wisely, stay away, and hoodlums roll citizens for some of the dollars they saved in taxes."

Galbraith did not so much want to abandon growth as to redirect it. Although heavily criticized by many economists, *The Affluent Society* established guideposts for the New Frontier and the Great Society. Operating within the reform tradition of Roosevelt, those administrations simultaneously applied the welfare and the training approaches to the poverty problem. Medicare was passed, social security payments were enlarged, minimum wage legislation was improved, housing legislation was added to, and the "war against poverty" was instituted.

Both Kennedy and Johnson saw the schools as important social instruments. Both presidents stressed the production instead of the consumption aspects of education. They viewed education in terms of national economic and military manpower needs and of human resource development. Both interpreted equality in terms of equality of opportunity.

The Economic Opportunity Act of 1964 was aimed primarily at eliminating poverty by training or retraining people who had been unable to get a job. One of the agencies created by the Act, the Job Corps, was designed to provide help to up to 100,000 young people whose background made them "least fit for useful work." Practical job training, work experience, and academic catch-up courses, among other things, were provided. To Johnson the camps were "new educational institutions, comparable in innovation to the land grant colleges." Work-training and Work-study programs were also set up to enable young people to finish school and university. Operation Head Start established nursery schools in deprived areas in order to help those children compete with more fortunate children in regular schooling. The Elementary and Secondary Education Act of 1965 had as one of its main provisions financial assistance for "culturally deprived" children. In all cases, education was seen as an escape from the mire of poverty—for those who took advantage of it.

Kennedy's and Johnson's principles were widely acceptable, particularly as enunciated by Johnson, and their policies tactically were good politics. Some economists, such as Leon H. Keyserling, argued that the problems of inequality and social injustice eventually would be solved by more economic growth. According to this argument, without an increased total it would be impossible to distribute more money to the poor. With a larger pie the individual slices would be larger, and even the smallest ones would be adequate. Other economists, such as Gunnar Myrdal, held that economic growth alone would not solve the problems. According to this view the problems could be solved only by related structural changes, notably by changes in access to education and in the articulation of education to employment opportunities. Kennedy's and Johnson's policies pleased both groups. Their emphasis on production showed the expansionists that they did not want to slow down economic growth; their emphasis on opportunity and manpower training pleased enough structuralists. Militarists were pleased by the link of education to military strength. Moreover, the explicit emphasis on education as production instead of as consumption and the continued adherence to the principle of equality of opportunity pleased conservatives, liberals, and various others who still gave ideological allegiance to inequality. Equality of opportunity combined with emphasis on production leads to inequality of class; equality of opportunity combined with emphasis on consumption comes precariously close to equality of status or equality of condition. The latter policy was still unacceptable.

The legislation passed by the Kennedy and Johnson administrations was inadequate when set against national needs and national capacities to provide a decent life for all. While there were benefits, the costs of the economic growth of the postwar years were high: unbalanced social development, inequities and disintegration, pollution, decayed and beleaguered cities, and not least of all, psychic strains. In the changed circumstances the traditional doctrine of equality of opportunity was more difficult to apply and had different consequences than heretofore.

Not all groups were content to reaffirm the old doctrines. A New Left radicalism developed. Informed by an eclectic moral idealism, it constituted, according to Jack Newfield, "an ethical revolt against the visible devils of racism, poverty and war, as well as the less tangible devils of centralized decision-making, manipulative, impersonal bureaucracies, and the hypocrisy that divides America's ideals from its actions...." This "prophetic minority," as Newfield called it, expressed its politics in "its affirmation of community, honesty, and freedom, and its indifference to ideology, discipline, economics, and conventional political forms." In 1962 the Students for a Democratic Society adopted the *Port Huron Statement*. Among other things it attacked both capitalism and the welfare state. It held that both "the liberal and socialist preachings of the past" were inadequate. The New Left advanced a radical, pluralistic egalitarianism and a communitarianism and sought to fuse them in its notion of "participatory democracy." Although ethically rooted, its politics in the early 1960s basically were to undertake piecemeal reform, to propose practical solutions to real-life problems. Arguing for political realignment both nationally and internationally, the New Left suggested the university as the agent for the desired social change. That is, it continued the tradition of Jefferson, Franklin, Mann, and Dewey of attributing to educational institutions power to effect broad social reform.

However, none of the modes of action initially used by the New Left—civil rights work, community, campus, and factory organizing, or electoral politics—was successful in bringing about change. The young failed to take control of the universities from their traditional managers. Moreover, their indifference to ideology, and their impatience with logical requirements, proved to be fatal flaws, because they failed to develop a theory that went beyond liberalism and socialism. By the late 1960s, the politics of the New Left were either clandestine and violent, such as those of the Weathermen, or inclined toward copping out from conventional political processes. For example, in 1970 in *Do It!* Jerry Rubin wrote: "Our politics is our music, our smell, our skin, our hair, our warm naked bodies, our drugs, our energy, our underground papers, our vision." This was a far cry from the "participatory democracy" of the *Port Huron Statement*. Reform, obviously needed, still had no theory to guide it.

Conventional politics were also undergoing stresses. The conflict and confusion of the Democratic Convention of 1968 were merely visible symptoms of deeper disorders. Political parties in the United States typically had been loose coalitions. The Democrats under Roosevelt put together a coalition, consisting of the South, the urban poor, labor unions, and intellectuals, that controlled the White House in the 1930s, 1940s, and 1960s. In the 1960s that coalition started falling apart. The party's strength in the South was challenged by George Wallace and by a Republican "Southern strategy" formulated by Senator Strom Thurmond of South Carolina and Richard M. Nixon, elected president in 1968. Organized labor in the 1960s spoke for comfortable Middle America, its goals shaped by the established power structure. Housed in the suburbs and afraid of change, union members moved politically to the right. Preoccupied with the chaos and uncertainty that characterized the 1960s, workers—Middle America in general—blamed university youth and blacks for the troubles and looked for simple solutions to the problems. Democratic and Republican "law and order" candidates for political office at the local, state, and national levels saw that order and inequality were linked, and thought they could secure the former without eliminating the latter.

Both national political parties were in flux. But new doctrines and new remedies were not readily available. The nation looked for means to make the old ones work better.

The Republican party took control of the White House in the presidential election of 1968 to "bring us together," as Nixon said. But the prospects for a major transformation of society by peaceful and democratic means remained dim. It seemed obvious that the problem was not solely, or even primarily, an economic one. The production of more goods and services alone could not solve the tragic social problems that had been allowed to accumulate. On the contrary, some analysts felt that continued emphasis on production would exacerbate the problem. There was already much wealth but little ease, enormous power but little confidence, great talent but little hope. In May 1970, the stock market dropped significantly. One analyst claimed the drop in the market was "not explicable in terms of weakness in the economy. It's a reflection that our society is coming apart." In the same year, John W. Gardner, former Secretary of Health, Education and Welfare, echoed the warning: "The nation disintegrates. I use the phrase soberly: the nation disintegrates." The 1960s opened with optimism but closed with despair.

chapter two

war, machines,
and education

On January 17, 1961, President Dwight D. Eisenhower delivered his Farewell Address. A remarkable and frequently cited document, it called attention to two immediate and serious threats to the nation. It deserves to be quoted at length. The first threat grew from felt defense needs. To meet these needs, Eisenhower said, the United States had been "compelled to create a permanent armaments industry of vast proportions. Added to this, three and a half million men and women are directly engaged in the defense establishment. . . .

"This conjunction of an immense military establishment and a large arms industry is new in the American experience. The total influence—economic, political, even spiritual—is felt in every city, every State house, every office of the Federal government. We recognize the imperative need for this development. Yet we must not fail to comprehend its grave implications. Our toil, resources and livelihood are all involved; so is the very structure of our society.

"In the councils of government, we must guard against the acquisition of unwarranted influence, whether sought or unsought, by the military-industrial complex. The potential for the disastrous use of misplaced power exists and will persist.

"We must never let the weight of this combination endanger our liberties or democratic processes. We should take nothing for granted. Only an alert and knowledgeable citizenry can compel the proper meshing of the huge industrial and military machinery of defense with our peaceful methods and goals, so that security and liberty may prosper together."

The second threat to which Eisenhower referred was related to the first. A technological revolution, he said, had created the need for "formalized, complex, and costly" research. The federal government was more and more involved in directing and financing it. Consequently, "the free university, historically the fountainhead of free ideas and scientific discovery, has experienced a revolution in the conduct of research. Partly because of the huge costs involved, a government contract becomes virtually a substitute for intellectual curiosity. . . .

"The prospect of domination of the nation's scholars by Federal employment, project allocations, and the power of money is ever present—and is gravely to be regarded." On the other hand, Eisenhower claimed that the nation needed to be "alert to the equal and opposite danger that public policy could itself become the captive of a scientific-technological elite."

The dangers to which Eisenhower referred—the pervasiveness of huge industrial and military machinery, the threat to democratic ideals, the possible distortion of teaching and of learning, and the threat of elitism (or technocracy)—were not all new. They were part of the development of modern America, the beginning of which, as we saw in the Introduction, Commager located in the 1890s. They merely intensified throughout the twentieth century, the awareness of their existence was heightened, and the consequences of permitting them to remain unchallenged were more obvious. Perhaps Eisenhower's geratest act as president was that he candidly and sincerely stated the threats; and because he was such a greatly respected and admired leader, he therefore made them credible to large numbers of people who ordinarily would have been unaware—or at best, vaguely aware—of their existence.

In any event, militarism, industrialism, and elitism were dominant themes in the period from 1918 to 1970.

The Military

As early as 1914 President Woodrow Wilson expressed an opinion about war and military defense that had meaning beyond the immediate circumstances in which it was given. A German victory in the war, he said, would compel the United States to "give up its present ideals and devote all its energies to defense, which would mean the end of its present system of government."

In 1970 President Richard Nixon said the world had not had a full generation of peace in the twentieth century.

Without too much exaggeration, the first 70 years of the century can be called an "age of total war." The century opened in the immediate aftermath of the expansionism and bombast of the Spanish-American War. Although American participation in World War I was short, the war dominated world attention, and its resolution permanently affected the course of world development.

In the 1920s, however, industrial prosperity and preoccupation with domestic affairs led the United States to reject a role of world leadership. In the 1930s, the Depression caused the nation to turn inward. Moreover, in the 1920s and 1930s the belief grew that the United States should not have entered World War I. Hemingway in *A Farewell To Arms* and John Dos Passos in his *U.S.A.* trilogy expressed disillusionment with world politics. The public had little interest in political or economic association with the rest of the world.

Nevertheless, European militarism affected American domestic responses. The Roosevelt administration saw a need for a strong foreign policy for the United States, but isolationists in Congress successfully opposed the administration and proceeded to pass neutrality legislation. In 1935 Congress forbade arms exports to nations at war. The next year it prohibited loans to belligerents. In 1938 it passed the Ludlow amendment to the Constitution, which tried to make it mandatory that the nation could enter a war only after a national referendum. In 1940, the "America First" organization emerged strongly and argued that traditional liberties could be lost in war and that democracy could be harmed permanently.

In Europe, German and Italian armaments and ambitions and in the Far East, Japan's expansion into China in the 1930s presented the nation with a choice between withdrawal from or participation in world events. After 1938 the nation paid more attention to the rest of the world.

In 1939 Roosevelt said that "when peace has been broken anywhere (the) peace of all countries everywhere is in danger." Peace was broken in 1939. The United States entered World War II in 1941, and it has been in some kind of war since: the Cold War of the 1950s and 1960s, the Korean War of the early 1950s, and the Viet Nam War of the 1960s.

More than merely unfortunate interruptions in normal national development, these wars had incalculable social, political, economic, and psychological consequences. During World War I the shipping and food production industries were bolstered. An aviation industry, which previously did not exist, was created to produce war planes. Whereas formerly the government had tried to maintain competition, during the war it engaged in economic planning and successfully controlled and coordinated industrial production.

Many features characteristic of postwar America were created between 1941 and 1945. Large strata of the population were mobilized and benefits were given to them in return. Part of the patriotic national establishment, organized labor increased its power and assured that its demands largely were met. Massive government spending for war production made possible and practicable the abolition of unemployment. At the end of 1939, 5½ million people were unemployed; by 1944 the figure had dropped to 670,000. Agricultural subsidies were begun. Business interests entered into war activities with financial encouragement from the government. Set in motion by the war, industrial production nearly doubled between 1940 and 1944. The enormous needs of the fighting forces were met. As a result of their wartime successes, business and industrial leaders were held in high esteem by the public. Their influence on government was strong.

A certain sense of community was created. Participation in war activities gave greater visibility to the accomplishments and abilities of groups such as the blacks, and it helped make them more confident and articulate in pressing their social demands. A spirit of bipartisan collaboration in foreign policy developed and continued unbroken through the Cold War, the Korean War, and the Viet Nam War. By uniting the population against outsiders, temporary meaning was given to many lives.

Of course, wars did not always encourage democratic or humane feelings. Quite apart from the unspeakable killing and destruction, they invariably brought forth an emotional expression that had tragically divisive consequences. The Viet Nam War in the 1960s was the most obvious example of this, but it was not unique to that war.

President Woodrow Wilson supposedly was aware of some of the insidious influences of war. In 1917 he allegedly said, "Once lead this people into war, and they'll forget there ever was such a thing as tolerance; to fight you must be brutal and ruthless, and the very spirit of ruthless brutality will enter into the very fiber of our national life." Fighting almost continuously since 1941, a black leader, Rap Brown, in the 1960s was able to say about the United States that "violence is as American as apple pie."

An ugly, destructive intolerance accompanied the wars. The hysteria of World War I encouraged some leaders to demand that a code of Americanism be inculcated and that everyone swear allegiance to it. Hatred was propogated by newspapers, schools, and churches. Recent immigrants were suspected; the use of foreign languages was discouraged. The public on the whole failed to make a distinction between political radicalism and pro-German feeling. Civil liberties were threatened. President Wilson sent Socialist leader Eugene Debs to jail, and his Attorney General, A. Mitchell Palmer, started the first American witch hunt after the Russian Revolution. Socialist periodicals such as *The Masses* and *The Milwaukee Leader* were forbidden use of the mails by the Post Office Department. The Department of Justice arrested persons suspected of radicalism, often with little or no legal justification.

Although all "alien" radical ideas were resisted, hostility was particularly directed toward communism. The Bolshevik government of Russia was not officially recognized by the United States government until 1933. Some state governments passed laws that declared Communist organizations illegal. State laws requiring loyalty oaths from teachers were instituted in the 1920s; more states enacted such laws after World War II. The Red mania was used early in the Depression as a political weapon against Roosevelt and the New Deal. The Cold War and the Korean War stirred anti-Red sentiment again, and in the early 1950s fed McCarthyism. The *New York Times* wrote at that time that "a subtle, creeping paralysis of freedom of thought" had set in.

World War II brought about a power revolution. Coupled with the rise to a position of power of Russia was the relative decline in power of England and Western Europe. In the 1950s there was an anticolonial revolution in the Third World of Asia, Africa, and Latin America. The United States was compelled to assume a new role. As Herbert Agar put it, in 1957 in *The Price of Power: America Since 1945*, it was "a nation no longer safe and self-contained but caught forever in the whirlpool of world politics."

In 1945 the United States had the classic attributes of power. Boasting 40 percent of the world's income, and with an enormous and recently successful military-industrial machine, it was able to use these resources to affect the behavior of other nations. An international perspective was needed. In the center of world affairs, there was nothing "we can argue any more," Agar wrote, "that is not afflicted with global interest."

But sadly the nation with the most power was one of the most poorly equipped to use it. According to Sir Winston Churchill, the United States in 1945 did not have a "true and coherent design" for world affairs. Finding the right formula for using its enormous power remained a problem for the nation for the quarter of a century after 1945. Neither the news media nor the schools were able to help much to shape an enlightened public opinion. The media, particularly newspapers, traditionally had a local focus; the schools had long been preoccupied with the narrow historical experience and cultural development of the United States. The isolationism of the interwar years also left the public unprepared for international responsibilities. The need to wed intelligence to power became all the more important when Russia developed hydrogen weapons in the 1950s, and when limitations were placed by friends and foes alike on both American military and economic power.

By 1947 the United States was locked in a Cold War with Russia. In July 1947 George Kennan wrote in *Foreign Affairs* that "the United States cannot expect in the foreseeable future to enjoy political intimacy with the Soviet regime. It must continue to regard the Soviet Union as a rival, not a partner, in the political arena." Kennan recommended that the United States follow "a policy of firm containment, designed to confront the Russians with unalterable counter-force at every point where they show signs of encroaching on the interests of a peaceful and stable world."

Neither the leaders nor the public were fitted by tradition or experience for the tasks at hand. What explicitly was intended as a policy of political confrontation and containment was turned into a military policy. A global design began to take shape. Countless civilian leaders, including President Truman and Secretary of State Dean Acheson, believed that "the American system" of freedom and prosperity could survive only if it expanded into a world system. Military leaders readily accepted this conception of social reality. This meant that throughout most of the 1940s, 1950s, and 1960s, the United States was once again a "mobilized society" geared to military and war preparedness. Political decisions were turned into military directives.

The "militarization of society" decisively affected the shape and quality of life. The monetary costs alone were gigantic. Late in 1940, Roosevelt had declared that America should be "the great arsenal of democracy." In that year he asked Congress for a combined total of nearly $3 billion for national defense. Congress granted the money with little opposition. It was a turning point in foreign and domestic history. For the next 30 years, at least, Congress gave virtually free rein to military spending on the premise that anything was acceptable in the name of national security. Military appropriations underwent monstrous growth; they increased from under $15 billion in 1950 to $80 billion in 1968, and there were no signs in 1970 that military spending would be reduced. In an address on "The War and Its Effects" to the United States Senate on December 13, 1967, Senator J. William Fulbright compared "the $904 billion we have spent on military power since World War II" with "the $96 billion we have spent, out of our regular national budget, on education, health, welfare, housing, and community development.

There were challenges to democratic theory and practice. Traditional arrangements were strained and distorted. During and for 25 years after World War II, business leaders were put in close association with military and civilian government leaders. Over this long period they were able to forge a close, semiofficial alliance. New mechanisms of cooperation and control emerged. In domestic and foreign affairs the defense conglomerate in effect was a "collateral government." It had influence over aspects of life that theoretically were reserved for the expression through political mechanisms of public opinion.

New jobs were created in defense and related industries; the practical interests and aspirations of millions of ordinary citizens were linked to military spending. In an important sense, domestic politics was an extension of military power and policies.

The Defense Department, not the State Department, effectively was in control of foreign policy. Anticommunism provided the ideology for the emerging American design for world affairs. Eisenhower, in his Farewell Address, said the nation faced "a hostile ideology—global in scope, atheistic in character, ruthless in purpose, and insidious in method." The conflict, he said, "commands our whole attention, absorbs our very beings." In 1967, Vice President Hubert Humphrey said that the nation had fought in Korea and Viet Nam to contain "militant, aggressive Asian Communism, with its headquarters in Peking, China."

The conventional view in America in the Cold War era was that the United States had no "narrow national interests" in the struggle; instead, it was a noble and disinterested power fighting for liberty around the world. President John F. Kennedy said Americans were "watchmen on the walls of world freedom." Even in the late 1960s American actions in Viet Nam were thought of by many Americans as part of a "general program of international good will." Although its beneficent policies were sometimes ineffective, even bumbling, America's intentions were said to be idealistic and virtuous. The Soviet Union, on the other hand, was thought to be an evil, purposeful, totalitarian- and effective-power intent on world domination.

Taken together these views produced what Senator Thurston Morton of Kentucky called the "psychedelic rhetoric" of the Cold War. For example, Secretary of State John Foster Dulles argued in the 1950s that in order to help "liberate" the "captive peoples behind the Iron Curtain," American foreign policy should go as close to the "brink of war" as possible without actually going to war. And because political issues had been turned into military ones, it was difficult to limit both the rhetoric and the objectives of the parties in the struggle. In a policy statement in 1961, the Air Force Association said, for example, "Freedom must bury Communism or be buried by Communism. Complete eradication of the Soviet Union must be our national goal, our obligation to all free people, our promise of hope to all who are not free." It was assumed that no one would willingly choose communism as a governing ideology. The Air Force Association said, "We are determined to back our words with action even at the risk of war. We seek not merely to preserve our freedoms, but to extend them." Clearly, America's warmheartedness was potentially murderous, as it turned out to be in Viet Nam in the 1960s.

This rhetorical language had little contact with nuclear reality. Implicit in it was the view that it was possible to win a war, that a victor could be identified, and that winning provided an ending. Military facts suggested otherwise.

In the 1960s opinion began to shift away from the earlier simple pieties. The debates that took place were well within a framework of American values and traditions, as Senator Fulbright pointed out in 1966 in *The Arrogance of Power*. "There are two Americas," he wrote. "One is the America of Lincoln and Adlai Stevenson: the other is the America of Teddy Roosevelt and the modern superpatriots. One is generous and humane, the other narrowly egotistical; one is self-critical, the other self-righteous; one is sensible, the other romantic; one is good humored, the other solemn; one is inquiring, the other pontificating; one is moderate, the other filled with passionate intensity; one is judicious and the other arrogant in the use of great power." In the 1960s, the first America became more vocal. A reexamination of former aims and assumptions was undertaken. The fears of world conquest by Russia, the secrecy and security fixations, the search for traitors, the compulsive sword rattling, the hostility toward left-wing influences, and the belief that "the American way of life" should be carried to other nations, even if against their wishes, were all questioned.

In general, the corrosive effects on society of "the warfare state" and the influences of industrialism were systematically scrutinized.

Industry

Their ascendency essentially undisputed, American industrialists fostered a "continuous revolution" nearly a century before Mao Tse tung and the Chinese Communists gave the phrase wide currency in the 1950s and 1960s. The unrelenting technological onslought that they brought about seriously challenged the inherited democratic social system and put it under severe strain. The industrial system basically was neutral about democracy; it was clear that it was able to survive in a variety of social and cultural settings. By the beginning of the twentieth century the moral and social simplicities of an agrarian society where everything seemed clearly in hand were gone. To preserve American democracy, major ideological and institutional adjustments were needed.

The American pragmatists under the intellectual leadership of Charles Sanders Peirce, William James, and John Dewey attempted to provide a rationale for the industrial changes of the nineteenth and twentieth centuries. They challenged accepted assumptions and practices and set out to forge new ones. Influenced by science, they sought to make their theories of the individual, society, and knowledge consistent with empirical methods. Instead of pessimistically withdrawing from the conditions of a scientific-industrial society, as many important thinkers did in England in the same period, the pragmatists, confident and optimistic, enthusiastically identified the machine with personal and social advancement. Values and standards, they said, were not opposed to everyday industrial society, but instead grew out of it and were conditioned by it.

The pragmatists rejected the dualistic view of the universe that held that there is a perfect, true, ideal universe in a separate sphere behind the phenomenal world of flux. The universe is not fixed, they said; it is in a constant state of change and "becoming."

They also rejected the notion of ultimate or universal truth. Truth and knowledge, they said, did not exist in a separate world of their own. To them, truth was never total, absolute, and certain; it was always fractional, arbitrary, and tentative. Knowledge was composed of hypotheses that had been or could be tested empirically. Rational and secular, it had value in so far as it was useful in attaining certain specific goals. An idea or belief was true, or had warranted assertability, if it had certain kinds of desirable effects within a specific set of circumstances. While there was no such thing as perfect knowledge, there were, they thought, tentative conclusions for which consensus could be reached.

The pragmatists rejected theories that divided man into higher and lower parts. Mind and body, thinking and feeling were not separate entities to them. Man, they said, was a unified organism with biological and social needs that he sought to satisfy. The body and the senses of man were not necessarily corrupting influences subordinate to the intellect; to the pragmatists, the senses helped provide data that could be used to decide on appropriate action. Man's personality was malleable, they said; it was influenced in part by the circumstances—social and physical—in which it was exhibited.

As there was no fixity in human nature, neither was there fixity in society. Individuals were claimed to be unique; they were not forced by their biological makeup, or by tradition, to be fitted into a preordained and fixed social class or category. Society, like the universe, was, to the pragmatists, in a state of continuous creation. Instead of denying or rejecting change, they accepted it and argued that it could be used by man to arrange the kind of society he wanted. They advocated an open society where men, individually and collectively, solved their problems through reflective thinking.

More than any other one man, John Dewey provided in philosophical terms a rationale specifically for education that took account of the processes of industrialization and mass democracy. He reiterated Jefferson's faith in the ability of the schools to enable citizens in a democracy to know their rights and to discharge their duties and responsibilities. But instead of the rural, agrarian society that Jefferson favored, Dewey recognized the inevitability of an urban-industrial society. He saw many of the conflicts and tensions in such a society. He was aware, for instance, that industrial processes threatened to exclude large numbers of people from the institutions and processes by which conventional democratic majorities were formed. However, he also saw, and chose to celebrate, the potential and the power of industrial civilization. With a reconstruction of American institutions, he said, it would be possible for people to continue to participate freely and justly in communal life.

He had a strong sense of community. He held that "democracy is more than a form of government; it is primarily a mode of associated living." To sustain an industrial, communitarian democracy, he saw that new assumptions and new practices were needed. Dewey placed less emphasis on the importance of an aristocracy of talent and more emphasis on mass participation through the release of organized intelligence than Jefferson did. However, both men, in their different ways, gave to the schools a central and distinctive role to play in social and political affairs. They held that the schools could help individuals and society by functioning partly as broad service agencies. If men could not be perfected, at least they could be modified by pedagogical procedures.

Dewey proposed that the schools take on functions performed in rural communities by other agencies such as the family, the church, and the town meeting. If community could be retained, he felt that it would be done through the schools. To this end he proposed a reformed intellectualism. He switched emphasis in teaching from subjects to personal and community needs. The curriculum, he said, should consist of problems of interest and significance to the pupils, and it should prepare them for intelligent social participation. A balanced, adjusted, self-regulating individual, aware of community needs and willing and able to solve the problems of the social order, was an objective of instruction.

Dewey rejected the dichotomy between liberal education and vocational training. He held, on the contrary, that vocational education could form the core of a general education. He did not want industrial education to emphasize narrow work efficiency. Instead he urged that it be informed by ethical and philosophical considerations. He thought that by starting with the immediate and the specific, instruction could move more effectively toward the abstract and the general. The pupil, through education for work, could be inducted into an understanding of the larger forces of production and of nature, which in turn would help him more successfully to solve the problems of industrial democracy. Moreover, he felt that such an education was more consistent with democracy than the inherited system, because it helped to break down the traditional invidious distinctions between work with the head and work with the hands, between a decorative and a functional education, between consumption of culture and production of necessities.

Circumstances determined the extent of influence the pragmatists had with their ideas in general and their educational views in particular. The managers of the new technology, sometimes acting from a set of assumptions different from the pragmatists, also made sense of the emerging society and fashioned institutional means by which they could control it.

With the growth of scientific technology, large sums of money were required to build factories, equip them, provide them with raw materials, and employ a labor force. Individual capitalists or even partnerships usually were unable to supply the necessary funds. The corporation was one answer. Industrial leaders gathered money from a great number of people and were thereby able to finance large-scale ventures. Machine technology, new sources of energy such as oil and electricity, a ready supply of capital, plentiful natural resources, and a labor supply combined to make mass production possible. Standardization of both parts and productive operations and specialization of labor were necessary ingredients of the system. On its own terms, the system was enormously successful. The twentieth century is the age of corporations; by 1960 nearly all manufacturing was done by them.

Technology and the corporate structure grew together. The interaction of men, machines, ideas, and organization created what John Kenneth Galbraith in 1967 in *The New Industrial State* called the "technostructure." The expansion of industry and the rise of corporations laid the foundations for a new power structure. These forces undercut the power of rural communities and shifted the locus of power from small-town lawyers, bankers, merchants, and editors to the enormous centralized and specialized bureaucracies and technocracies of the new industrial system.

Once introduced into a culture, institutions have a logic and set of imperatives of their own. The corporate structure was no exception. Obviously corporations changed the structure and operation of the economy, but their assumptions and mode of operations had an influence far beyond the economic sphere. They defined rules, roles, and values for the larger social system, and fixed the means by which and the degree to which it could be reformed.

Max Weber, in his study of bureaucracies, characterized their authority as being "legal-rational." In the purest type of bureaucratic organization each office has carefully defined functions organized hierarchically. Appointment and promotion are governed by public and rational criteria such as technical qualifications, seniority, and/or achievement. The people filling the offices are paid in money for their services and are subject to an agreed on authority.

Weber's model of bureaucracy was influenced by the organization of the Prussian army. Before and during World War I the German army was considered the paradigm of efficient organization. In modern states civil and military bureaucracies grew together, and the influence of the latter on the former has been considerable.

Business organization and administration, for example, were influenced by military practices, and it would be difficult to exaggerate the pervasiveness of business in America and its impact, in turn, on government administration. "Keep government out of business" was a cry heard from the founding of the Republic in the eighteenth century. By the twentieth century the cry was "More business in government." As early as 1887 Woodrow Wilson wrote that, "The field of administration is a field of business." In 1924 William Redfield in *With Congress and Cabinet* was more enthusiastic and more detailed: "Do you ask just what government departments are? I reply that in general they are great business establishments running factories, buying goods, distributing products, employing workmen of many kinds, engaged in guiding, navigating, traveling, research, publication, farming, instruction, and in almost every kind of production activity." It is interesting to note parenthetically that as early as the 1920s research and instruction were considered business activities. Evidently the threat of the military-industrial complex to education did not arise only in the 1950s or 1960s.

Although business suffered some loss of prestige during the 1930s, business leaders regained their morale and confidence during and after World War II. Business influences on public administration continued unabated from that time. In his reorganization of the government bureaucracy in June 1970, during which he created the Office of Budget and Management, President Nixon said that his administration was "finally bringing real business management" into government at the highest levels. Different kinds of administration continued to converge to conformity with the business model.

The design, structure, and operation of machines deeply influenced social, political, and economic life. Mechanical metaphors were widely used. In 1956 in *Perspectives on Administration*, Dwight Waldo suggested that the concept of social efficiency was a product of mechanical metaphor. "Achieving efficiency in administration," he said, "is conceived analogously to achieving efficiency in machine performance. There must be good design—organization charts equal blueprints—parts must be adjusted properly one to another; friction must be reduced; power loss prevented, and so forth." The attachment to the machine was so pronounced that it was one of the "root metaphors" throughout the twentieth century. Even in the 1960s when many Americans started seeing society in terms of an electronic system (the "technetronic" society), the machine metaphor was not abandoned.

The emergent technological society was technique and management intensive. By the 1960s Galbraith argued that "the decisive power in the modern industrial society is exercised not by capital but by organization." Technological efficiency was the main purpose toward which society was directed.

Modern social and economic organization thus came to be based on cooperative enterprise, but of a special kind. It was close, but not, of course, identical, to the social arrangements elucidated by the conservative theory of society and social justice, the kind advocated by Plato in the *Republic*. There was a hierarchy of narrowly defined, specialized functions; social power descended from an elite; stress was on obedience, loyalty, efficiency.

This event pointed out one of the developmental contradictions of corporate capitalism: it was technologically bold and innovative, but socially and morally conservative. Although the vast economic system and giant corporations actually restricted individual liberty and suggested the need for a countervailing power, the widespread and vigorous advocacy of the ideology of *laissez faire* insured that there was little untoward government interference in economic affairs. In the face of the institutional reality conservatives and liberals alike still preferred the norms of liberty over equality and individualism over community. Under the circumstances the emphasis on these norms had the consequence of making the individual extremely vulnerable to corporate control. When government intervened, it was to help improve the conditions under which the contest doctrine of equality of opportunity operated. The entrepreneurial path to upward mobility decreased in importance, but promotion through corporate hierarchies increased in importance. Although the contest norm of social mobility remained ascendant, the emerging institutional structure made possible an easy shift to sponsored mobility thinking. Conant moved in this direction in his recommendations for the high school. In any case, in the context of corporate capitalism, both norms guaranteed the continuation of great inequalities.

It was frequently remarked how daring American capitalism was. Supporters and detractors alike referred to its commitment to change, to novelty, to new products, and to new processes. It was less frequently pointed out that the change was narrowly prescribed. Adaptable, technique-oriented people were needed, but changes that opposed the needs of the technostructure were discouraged.

The technostructure itself was not amenable to rapid change. The large organizations that had developed typically did not—and if they wanted to perpetuate their power, could not—accommodate themselves readily to change. They were designed to be buffered from rapid and unforeseen changes. Early in the century investment bankers assumed some responsibility for the management as well as for the financing of the new corporate enterprises. Through interlocking directorships they created a "community of interests," a means by which they prevented undesirable consequences from unchecked competition, a habit of mind that persisted into the post-World War II military-industrial complex to which Eisenhower referred. Changes consistent with the needs of the organizations were selectively absorbed.

The task of altering the system grew in difficulty as the bureaucracies—government, business, military, and educational—became more and more interrelated. The strength of the technostructure and the nature of its needs were clearly exhibited in the 1960s. In the context of unprecedented wealth, the tremendous difficulties encountered in creating a just society—by eliminating poverty, reducing humiliating class differences, and providing a minimum of security through health and welfare services—were measures of the power of the system to resist change and of its reliance on insecurity and inequality. In July 1969, in an analysis of the social impact of technology in the *New York Review of Books*, John McDermott claimed that "... the new technology, celebrated ... for its potential contributions to democracy, contributes instead to the errosion of that same democratic ethos. For if, in an earlier time, the gap between the political cultures of the higher and lower orders of society was being widely attacked and closed, this no longer appears to be the case. On the contrary, I am persuaded that the direction has been reversed and that we now observe evidence of a growing separation between ruling and lower-class culture in America, a separation which is particularly enhanced by the rapid growth of technology and the spreading influence of its *laissez innover* ideologues."

The challenge of the institutions of the technostructure to received economic and political ideas was pointed out in 1932 by A. A. Berle, Jr. and Gardiner C. Means in *The Modern Corporation and Private Property*. One of the distinctive features of corporate growth of the 1920s was the separation of the ownership of capital from the management of business. Power switched to the latter. The movement toward management control constituted a minor revolution, according to Berle and Means. The separation destroyed, they said, "the very foundation on which the economic order of the past three centuries has rested." It also destroyed "the basis of the old assumption that the quest for profits will spur the owner of industrial property to its effective use. It consequently challenges the fundamental economic principle of individual initiative in industrial enterprise." This claim raised the issue of whether the managers were more concerned with profits or with power.

The dissolution of property into ownership and control gave

to the managers of the new specialized bureaucracies enormous prestige and a power that went beyond economic power alone. In 1942, James Burnham in *The Managerial Revolution* saw them as a new ruling class. The nature of the elites, their objectives, and the means by which they were selected were vital national issues, particularly in the 1960s.

One of the supporters of elite control and of sponsored mobility was Zbigniew Brzezinski. Writing in *The New Republic* in December 1967, he indicated some of the broader social implications of "meritocracy." He held that the emerging "technetronic society" would be characterized by the application of "... the principle of equal opportunity for all but ... special opportunity for the singularly talented few." This society, he said, would combine "... continued respect for the popular will with an increasing role in the key decision-making institutions of individuals with special intellectual and scientific attainments." Brzezinski foresaw that "The educational and social systems (would make) it increasingly attractive and easy for those meritocratic few to develop to the fullest of their special potential."

Not all students of society were as optimistic as Brzezinski; nor were all as ready to accept bureaucracy and meritocratic control. As we saw in Chapter One, the Students for a Democratic Society in their *Port Huron Statement* rejected it in the early 1960s. Nor were all willing to accept uncritically the consequences of following the doctrine of equality of opportunity. The mobility system is functionally related to other subsystems —to the family, to education, and to the occupational structure—and there were some doubts about whether equality of opportunity was consistent with other professed social aims. John McDermott, for example, argued that to the new scientific and technical managerial elites the principle of equality of opportunity "has precious little to do with creating a more egalitarian society. On the contrary," he said, "it functions as an indispensible feature of the highly stratified society they envision for the future. For in their society of meritocratic hierarchy, equality of opportunity assures that talented young meritocrats ... will be able to climb into the 'key decision-making' slots reserved for trained talent, and thus generate the success of the new society, and its cohesion. . . ."

According to Brzezinski, the managers of the system, burdened with decision making, would need to undergo continuous retraining. The rest, however, could develop ". . . interest in the cultural and humanistic aspects of life, in addition to purely hedonistic preoccupations." The latter, he said, "would serve as a social valve, reducing tensions and political frustrations."

A problem for this theory remained, however: what to do with the superfluous hedonistic consumers of culture. In May 1970, two political scientists, John H. Schaar and Sheldon S. Wolin, foresaw one possibility. In "Where We Are Now," in the *New York Review of Books*, they wrote: "The governors of the technological order could combine repressive measures with a welfare system which would produce euphoric demoralization. Such a welfare system would merely have to extend many elements already present or probable, such as a guaranteed annual income and unemployment compensation. Subsidize the arts so that music would blare throughout the land, and then take the final step of relaxing drug controls." In a curious way, the politics of Jerry Rubin in 1970 were not far from this policy option of the managers of the technostructure. The incredible was credible.

Euphoria was not experienced by many Americans in the first 70 years of the twentieth century. Efficiency and economic expansion were given higher priority than social welfare legislation. More than in any other nation, the quality of life was shaped by technology and the institutions that served it. The social and psychic costs were high. Symbols and values from the past, if not consistent with technology, were likely to be abandoned; hopes frequently were shattered. Capacity for community was weakened or destroyed by the bureaucracies created to serve technology. Cooperation was exploited. The mode of organization of the bureaucracies—the specialized functions, the impersonal manner of operation, and the hierarchical arrangements—acted as a dehumanizing force, as Max Weber foresaw. Problems of identity and alienation—the estrangement of man from man—were heightened. Rigidification of society set in. Conflicting interests and loyalties developed, an issue discussed by William H. Whyte in *The Organization Man*, one of the widely discussed social critiques of the 1950s.

In general, technology denied personal fulfillment in work activities. Work in factories was uncreative, routinized, and unadventurous. Men were machine tenders with little fun or significance in what they did. Salaried employees and professional people steadily increased their importance in the labor force throughout the century, but even they could not always look forward to involvement and to challenging and rewarding work. Both industrial workers and the salariat had what Marc A. Fried writing in *Transaction* in September/October 1966 called a job: the worker had to "learn to work with and be subordinate to other people." Few had an occupation where they could "begin to develop responsibility for and identity with, an entire work objective, an over-all integrated goal...." Fewer still had what Fried called a career, where they could identify "their own personal achievement—often much of their total personalities—with their occupation." Only the managers of the technostructure could have careers and find self-fulfillment through work.

In the 1960s, college students tried to take hold of their own work futures. In 1962 the *Port Huron Statement* of the Students for a Democratic Society said in part "... that work should involve incentives worthier than money or survival. It should be educative, not stultifying; creative, not mechanical; self-direct, not manipulated; encouraging independence, a respect for others, a sense of dignity and a willingness to accept social responsibility, since it is this experience that has crucial influence on habits, perceptions and individual ethics...." The "back to the farm" and the commune movements of the 1960s were in part quiet and harmless rejections of the nature of work and of many of the values of the larger system. The craft movement was revitalized in the 1960s and stressed a quality of workmenship and attention to detail that had been destroyed by the mainstream of production.

However, by 1970 there was little room for optimism about the possibility of any significant changes occurring in the nature of work. No amount of psychological or sociological manipulation seemed to offer prospects for improvement. Perceptive students of society saw the Seventies as offering more of the same. In 1970, John Holt in an essay entitled "Education for the Future," wrote: "What sort of things make a man feel unfree? One is being pushed around: having to submit to other men whom he cannot reach, see, or talk to, and over whom he feels he has no control. Another is not knowing what goes on, feeling that he is not told, and cannot find, the truth. Still another is feeling that he has no real say about his own life, no real choices to make; that the decisions that determine whether he goes this way or that are made by other men, behind his back. The great danger to freedom in this society lies in the fact that the objective conditions that make men feel this way are increasing and are sure to continue to increase."

Education

Education theory and practice did not remain free from the influence of government or industry. Indeed, universal schooling developed as an important agency in the movement to incorporate everybody into the industrial state. The politicalization of education in its modern form was advocated in the eighteenth century in France by such revolutionary thinkers as Condorcet and was continued in the United States. Jefferson, Franklin, and Mann saw the schools as instruments for achieving desired social ends. Dewey continued this tradition in the twentieth century.

The belief in the power of education worked its way up the educational system. From approximately 1840 to 1918 attention was centered on the elementary schools. With the virtual achievement of universal elementary education by 1918, educationists turned their attention to the secondary schools and attributed great socializing powers to them. As large numbers of youngsters continued to the universities, beginning roughly in 1945, the unbounded faith in the power of education to cure all social ills was extended to include them. Thus, over a period of two centuries the whole educational system was fused into a national instrument with broad social, political, and economic objectives.

Defining education as a means of social control meant that schools and universities were deeply and continuously involved in political power struggles. By trying to be "all things to all men," the schools not only lost sight of any clear purpose for themselves, they also assured that control over them went to the most powerful groups in the nation. In the twentieth century this meant the schools and universities served the interests of the technostructure and of the national state.

It was not always easy to see the differences between the interests and the needs of these two power blocs. The federal government had been continuously active in American economic growth. In 1962 Edmund S. Phelps in *The Goal of Economic Growth* pointed this out clearly. "Since Hamilton's first report on manufactures," he wrote, "this country has not let decisions affecting economic growth be made exclusively by private individuals and groups. Our tariff history, the patent laws, the homestead act, the land grants to railroads, the establishment of numerous government agencies to help private industry to prosper and grow, the public development of land and water resources in many areas, public support of education and research—all these testify to the large role that public agencies have played in our growth." Powerful private interests frequently controlled government and directed it toward their ends.

The interests of industry and the state in education often were identical, or at least similar. In any case, the industrial system acted either directly or through the agency of the federal government to adapt education to its requirements. Schools and universities were seen as authority- and consensus-building agencies. They were given the task of cultivating in young people the attitudes, values, and skills that both the nation-state and the technostructure required for their continued power. Obedience, loyalty, efficiency, dedication, and order served the interests of both the political and the economic systems. The schools taught them and they thereby legitimized those systems.

A respected and powerful rationale for turning the schools toward these conservative nationalistic objectives and for aligning them with the economic establishment came from a source that probably did not intend those exact consequences: the pragmatic educational philosophy of John Dewey. Out of Dewey's work, two strong curriculum movements had emerged. A child-centered curriculum gave priority to the interests and psychological needs of the individual child. A society-centered curriculum had as its organizing principle the problems of democratic society. On the whole, progressive educationists supported both approaches to the curriculum and held them in uneasy balance. Paradoxically, while both were intended as progressive and liberating doctrines, the consequences of their application in the context of the technostructure were conservative, even reactionary.

This was implicit in the social gospel that Dewey and other progressives taught. Dewey wanted to preserve the life and the values of traditional American democracy. He affirmed community and thought that the schools should help form "a socialized disposition." He argued that the schools should be close to life and that they should enable youngsters to "adjust to the environment." He wanted children to perceive "the essential interdependence" of industrial civilization and to appreciate their place on the industrial team.

In an environment dominated by the interests of the bureau-cratic institutions of the technostructure, there was little the schools could do but serve those interests. The models of authority that prevailed in the schools were derived from military and corporate models. "Law-respecting and law-abiding citizens" imbued with "the spirit of patriotism" and with "the habits of obedience" were the aims of education. Consequently, Dewey's theories about education for work were debased to serve primarily industrial manpower instead of individual educational needs. Education for cooperative living became education for life in the technostructure. As Paul Goodman put it, "Democratic community became astoundingly interpreted as conformity, instead of being the matrix of social experience and political change."

The schools influenced every citizen-worker, and as the century went on they did so for an increased number of years. The technostructure was, in Galbraith's phrase, "a consumer of men." In the early stages of industrialism, a man, through ability, desire, hard work, endurance, and perseverance, could advance in his work. A degree or certificate from a school or college was not a necessity. Andrew Carnegie, at least, thought such qualities more important for success than the reflective life provided by the universities. The complex technological society that developed, however, required a high degree of control over the skills, training, mobility, and attitudes of the work force. In order to plan its operations, the technostructure required a guaranteed supply of manpower with trained, disciplined intelligence. There was an increase in work specialties; extensive prior training in formal educational institutions, frequently extending over many years, was a prerequisite for many positions, particularly the attractive ones.

The "credential society" that emerged tended to be rather callous toward the untrained. In a cruel way they were considered human fallout. Motivating the future workers to stay in school and to undergo the lengthy training was a persistent problem for industry and for the educational system. The holding power of the schools and the problem of dropouts was widely discussed, particularly in the 1950s and 1960s. New and more powerful incentives were searched for, but finding them proved to be a difficult task. The incentive system had long been dominated by monetary rewards. As we have seen, the New Left in the 1960s called for a reformed set of incentives. The attempt was unsuccessful; monetary rewards retained their central position.

Although it was generally accepted that a wide diffusion of education was necessary for industrial success and for national development, this was not taken to mean either common or equal education for all. There was a technological underclass, ranging from the poorly trained to the well trained, and a meritocracy to control it. From a generally well-educated populace, theoretically, a few were expected to climb to the highest positions. Charles W. Eliot, reforming president of Harvard University and first honorary president of the Progressive Education Association, held this Jeffersonian view. Eliot believed that "the democracy must learn in governmental affairs to employ experts and abide by their decisions." As early as 1908 he was urging the schools to help discover and prepare this elite about which Eisenhower gave us warning a little over a half century later. "Here we come upon a new function for the teachers in our elementary schools," he said, "and in my judgment they have no function more important. The teachers of the elementary schools ought to sort the pupils, and sort them by their evident or probable destinies." The experts then putting the industrial system together, because they had different "destinies" and different "roles" from the industrial masses, allegedly needed a different education from the masses. The former needed a liberating education, the latter an "industrial education," which, under the circumstances, meant an education for a specific manual task.

The hierarchy of jobs and occupations was reflected in a hierarchy in education: different life roles called for differentiated education. In practice this meant that education was unequally distributed, a fact that had to be reconciled with democracy. The concept of a child-centered education based on a doctrine of individual differences provided a rationale for "differentiated education." Differences in capacities, aptitudes, and interests, it was claimed, were great enough to warrant organizing instruction around them. For instance, Jane Addams early in the century called on the schools to "make the course of study fit the child." Dewey and G. Stanley Hall, as we saw, also urged this policy.

But in an industrial context the child-centered doctrine was essentially conservative. In the terms of the medical model that progressive educators used frequently, it was not at all clear how "normal," "mature," and "well-adjusted" individuals would automatically produce a "healthy" society. Child-centered theorists had no better explanation about how the distance between the individual and the community was to be bridged than did liberal political or private enterprise theorists. The privatization of the curriculum made knowledge more unshareable and reduced its collective power; Eliot's elective system, which he introduced at Harvard in the nineteenth century, served the same end. The antiintellectual emphasis on "doing" instead of on "knowing" also acted to deter a systematic and critical inquiry into the workings of society and the distribution of power in it. Such tendencies helped render both the schools and the individuals in them impotent in the face of powerful external interests.

Despite disclaimers and statements of objectives to the contrary, there was an obvious discrepancy between talk about individualized instruction and education for civic and industrial objectives. Frequently the needs of the individual were equated with the needs, not of society, but of economic and political interests. The machinery of efficiency took over. Learning was graded by ages, subject matter was divided into courses. Children systematically were classified and put into groups according to capacities, aptitudes, interests and the work for which they were best fitted. In 1961 in *Slums and Suburbs* James Bryant Conant made this function explicit.

"I submit," he wrote, "that in a heavily urbanized and industrialized free society, the educational experiences of youth should fit their subsequent employment." Guidance personnel and an elaborate system of tests were used for this purpose, as we will see in the next chapter.

American educators rejected the European pattern of operating several different kinds of secondary schools, each devoted to a specific function, for example, academic, technical, commercial, and general. Instead, they put these different functions under one roof in a comprehensive secondary school. Conant's report in the 1950s on the high school reaffirmed this policy.

The comprehensive arrangement muted but did not, of course, completely eliminate the effects of the stratifying functions of the schools. Whether called "Pussycats" and "Bunnies," "Bluebirds" or "Sparrows," the different tracks in the comprehensive school did not have parity of esteem; prestige was attached to the ones that fed the most youngsters into colleges and universities and, through them, into high-class and status positions. The schools were part of the structure of control and domination. The doctrine of equality of opportunity helped legitimize both the educational and the social differences.

Seeing students as producers was explicit in two of the most influential statements of the purposes of education made by the Educational Policies Commission of the National Education Association. In 1938 in *The Purposes of Education in American Democracy* the Commission listed self-realization, human relationships, economic efficiency, and civic responsibility as specific objectives of instruction. The educated producer was one desired "concrete outcome" of the aim of economic efficiency. The educated producer, the report said, "knows the satisfaction of good workmanship, understands the requirements and opportunities for various jobs, has selected his occupation, succeeds in his chosen vocation, maintains and improves his efficiency, and appreciates the social value of his work."

In 1944 in *Education for All American Youth* the Commission continued to give emphasis to education for production. "All youth," the Commission said, "need to develop salable skills and those understandings and attitudes that make the worker an intelligent and productive participant in economic life. To this end, most youth need supervised work experience as well as education in the skills and knowledge of their occupations." The emphasis on production was continued in the 1950s and 1960s, particularly by the educational legislation of the Kennedy and Johnson administrations.

These reports and the educational system in general served the industrial system in another significant way. The drive to produce was determined by the ability and willingness to consume. The former was limitless if the latter could be so made. Consumer demand needed to be controlled. A powerful and pervasive advertising industry was developed to help shape patterns of consumption. This in turn produced what critics in the 1950s and 1960s called a "technology of false needs." The schools were also used as instruments of this form of social engineering. In *The Purposes of Education in American Democracy*, the Education Policies Commission placed the educated consumer beside the educated producer as one of the desired behaviors of economic efficiency. The educated consumer, the Commission said, "plans the economics of his own life, develops standards for guiding his expenditures, is an informed and skillful buyer, and takes appropriate measures to safeguard his interests." In *Education for All American Youth* the Commission asserted that "All youth need to know how to purchase and use goods and services intelligently, understanding both the values received by the consumer and the economic consequences of their acts." Clearly, schools were not seen as luxury institutions, "against the market." They functioned closely in relation to the economic and class system.

The system of higher education through its applied research activities and its professional training programs also functioned as an integral part of the industrial system. Although the links of universities to the military-industrial complex became obvious after World War II, they had long been used as instruments of economic growth. The foundations of the modern university were laid in the nineteenth century. Vocationalism in higher education was initiated in 1862 by the Morrill Land Grant Act, which set aside millions of acres of public land for the support of agricultural and industrial colleges. The modern graduate research and professional university took shape in the 1880s with the founding of Johns Hopkins and Clark universities. By the turn of the twentieth century, few policy makers for higher education in the United States would have agreed with T. H. Huxley's view, expressed in 1892, that "the primary business of the universities is with pure knowledge and pure art—independent of all application to practice; with progress in culture not with increase in wealth."

Either directly or through the state higher education was drawn into the technostructure. As early as the 1930s the universities had merged their purposes and structure with government and the corporate world. In 1968, James A. Perkins, president of Cornell University, recalled the intentions of the social revolutionaries of the 1930s. "Our dream," he said, "was that these four great social powers—business, labor, government, and the university—should work in some kind of balance toward the public good. The intellectual in government would assure wise public policy. Government working alongside business would curb the profit motive with public objectives. The bargaining between management and labor, monitored by government, would lead to higher wages, better working conditions, and a stable national income." Social planning and social change directed by liberal and enlightened experts seemed possible.

A slight countermovement started in the 1930s. The Depression encouraged a feeling of community, and in the colleges and universities there was a return to prescribed courses. World War II also made obvious a need for shared values. In 1945 the Harvard report entitled *General Education in a Free*

Society declared that the supreme purpose of secondary and higher education was to develop a common culture. The report made a distinction between "general" and "special" education. "General education," it said, is "that part of a student's whole education which looks first of all to his life as a responsible human being and citizen." Study in the natural and social sciences and the humanities, the report said, was the means by which the main traits of a general education could be achieved —effective thinking, communication skills, ability to make relative judgments, and discretion between values. According to the report, "special education" is "that part which looks to the student's competence in some occupation." The primary function of education, it said, was to help develop enlightened individuals; the secondary function was to produce specialized workers.

The secondary function became ascendant. In *The Organization Man* William H. Whyte claimed that by the 1950s practicalism and the social ethic dominated the curriculum and instruction of the universities. There was, he said, a decline in the number of students studying the traditional academic disciplines and an increase in the number of them in applied vocational fields. In 1963 in *The Uses of the University*, Clark Kerr, then president of the University of California, was able to celebrate the practical contributions of the "multiversity" to government and to business.

These educational responses were thought of by university officials and faculties, in part at least, as extensions of the old public service tradition. They assumed that the universities could serve national political and economic interests, as they had served local and state interests, without compromising either their neutrality or their freedom.

This assumption was challenged in the 1960s. Universities had undertaken to do useful work for the public at a time when both government and corporations were relatively weak. The public service doctrine did not take into account the mighty and sustained drive toward economic expansion during and after World War II, nor did it take into account the prolonged global Cold War, the hot war in Korea, and the lengthy and repugnant war in Viet Nam in the 1950s and 1960s. Under these conditions the state and the technostructure amassed tremendous power. Educated manpower was seen as a resource in the military and economic struggles. Universities were expanded to supply it.

Following the pattern of the factory and the army, the curriculum was standardized and power was bureaucratized in order to handle the technological complexity and the increased number of students. However, while the universities had grown in size and scope of operations, they had diminished in authority.

In the 1960s there was a national "crisis of confidence" in the universities. Critics asserted that the state and the technostructure had used the universities to help organize society for their own ideological and economic advantage. They claimed, moreover, that to get money, universities had joined the military-industrial complex instead of resisting it. The result, according to Senator Fulbright in his speech to the Senate, was "the surrender of independence, the neglect of teaching, and the distortion of scholarship." By becoming an "appendage to the government," critics said, the universities had betrayed a public trust, particularly their responsibilities to the students.

For their part, students "deauthorized" many of the values —such as responsibility, duty, patriotism, and good citizenship—toward which the schools had for so long earnestly and enthusiastically directed their attentions. They rejected Free World propaganda. The belief in American purity and omnipotence was found wanting. America was seen as an imperial power, acting in self-interest, and playing power politics to support its investments and its spheres of influence.

The Viet Nam War was particularly disruptive. Throughout most of the 1960s, apart from victory statements that were delivered regularly each week, government officials told the public less and less about what was going on. In time, a "credibility gap" developed. Students, along with much of the rest of the public, reached a point where they could not believe anything anybody told them. They resented, as they said, "that authoritative lying by which the world is run." A soldier in Viet Nam painted on his helmet a sentence that caught the complexity of feelings about the war there: "We are the unwilling, led by the unqualified, doing the unnecessary, for the ungrateful."

To the students, the whole educational system was a service organization directed toward the mass production of docile workers and technocrats. Conformity was equated with liberty, they said, and high consumption was equated with freedom. They rejected the limited aspirations and the narrowly defined roles set for them by the system. They "delegitimized" many received forms of power and control, and this shocked the public. As Perkins put it, "We worked hard during the '30's and '40's to bring (business, labor, government and the university) to some kind of understanding. . . . So it comes as a mean blow to discover that our successors now view our painstaking, hard-won collaboration as one vast, interlocking conspiracy. . . ."

As in the 1930s, students and social reformers in the 1960s worked hard to alter and to improve the system. But unlike the 1930s they were not successful in achieving their stated ends. Shocked and angered, the public resisted reform, sometimes violently. Unsuccessful, youth politics at the end of the 1960s reflected "desperation and exhaustion." As we saw in the last chapter, the "freak out" or the "cop out" seemed to be the only choices open to them. This led John H. Schaar and Sheldon S. Wolin to write, "The swift, savage years of the Sixties may come to be seen as the time when America said 'no' to much of the best that was herself."

The kind of social order that Perkins and others worked for in the 1930s, 1940s, and 1950s, and the kind that was rejected by the young in the 1960s was shaped primarily by the ideology and politics of liberalism. Under the auspices of liberal politicians and educationists, vocationalism and professionalism in education had unabated growth. The educational system had been so thoroughly permeated by the techniques, ethics, and aims of the industrial system that there were doubts whether the schools could free themselves from it, or even whether they could question it. A "free education from schooling" movement started. There was widespread doubt, from left and right alike, whether the traditional liberalism could continue to dominate politics. Many critics doubted that it should. By 1970, Philip E. Slater in *The Pursuit of Loneliness* decided that it could not be a good society if it made large numbers of people helpless or impotent.

"My main argument for rejecting the old culture," he wrote, "is that it has been unable to keep any of the promises that have sustained it for so long, and as it struggles more and more violently to maintain itself, it is less and less able to hide its fundamental antipathy to human life and human satisfaction. It spends hundreds of billions of dollars to find ways of killing more efficiently, but almost nothing to enhance the joys of living.... The old culture is unable to stop killing people—deliberately in the case of those who oppose it, with bureaucratic indifference in the case of those who obey its dictates or consume its products trustingly. However familiar and comfortable it may seem, the old culture is threatening to kill us...."

chapter three
intelligence testing and the efficient society

the attempt to measure something called native intelligence during the twentieth century has had profound impact on schools and the concept of the relationship of the schools to a democratic society. The term "native intelligence" implied an inborn mental capacity that was the result of inheritance instead of educational training. The idea of an inherited mental capacity introduced a certain amount of pessimism about the effectiveness of education in improving individual abilities. In 1939 Edward L. Thorndike, one of the leaders of the testing movement, argued that educational evangelists who hoped to reform the world through schooling were chasing a false dream. "If one has imagined," he wrote, "that ... the genes of a 'dull normal' ... [could] develop into a mind able to graduate from a reputable law school, he will be disappointed to learn that differences in home life and training probably cause less than a fifth of the variation among individuals in I.Q."

The belief in an inherited mental capacity also raised serious questions about the nature of a democratic society. The measurement of intelligence rested on the fundamental premise that all men were not born equal, nor was it possible to make them equal. This suggested that the dream of an egalitarian democracy rested on false assumptions. All men did not have equal ability to rule, nor could they equally participate in the effective running of government. Therefore it was quite logical for those who accepted the assumptions of the testing movement to argue that the exercise of political rights should depend on the level of intelligence. Henry H. Goddard, the pioneer in special education programs in the United States and the man primarily responsible for introducing to this country the intelligence test developed by French psychologist Alfred Binet, argued in 1920 that the franchise should be limited and those classified by intelligence tests as feeble minded should not be allowed to vote. This was a suggestion picked up by many states, and laws were passed to limit the franchise on the basis of level of intelligence.

While the developers of intelligence tests raised serious questions about the school and democracy, they did not dismiss them, but instead redefined their functions. The underlying dream of the testing movement was the creation of a society where everyone would do what he was best able to do. The role of intelligence tests was to sort people properly into social roles that matched their intellectual capabilities. Alfred Binet wrote in the early twentieth century that intelligence tests could create a "future where the social sphere would be better organized than ours; where every one would work according to his known aptitudes in such a way that no particle of psychic force should be lost for society." In the United States Goddard echoed Binet in arguing "that a perfect democracy is only to be realized when it is based upon an absolute knowledge of mental levels and the organization of the social body on that basis."

The role of the school within the context of this dream of the good society was the early sorting and classification of children. Mental tests would be used to determine what the child should study. If the student had a low intelligence score he would not be given a college preparatory course, but one more suited to his probable social destination, for example, a commercial or technical course. The problem for the schools was not more education, but education geared to the intellectual level of the student. Education would not reform society by making all men moral, as Horace Mann had hoped, but by aiding in the creation of an efficient social machine. The schools would act to channel manpower into proper social niches and would become the primary instruments for social selection.

This idea of the role of the school was intimately linked to the concept of democracy that emerged from the testing movement. Democracy within this context meant a form of social organization that allowed men the freedom to attain a social position that matched their intellectual abilities.

The schools were to be primary instruments in maintaining this form of democracy by assuring that each individual would be given the opportunity to achieve his level of competence. The schools would also assure through proper classification that only the qualified would become leaders of society.

Implied in this conception of democracy was a strong elitist idea that only the best or most intelligent should rule. Goddard saw the major problem for a democracy as convincing those with lower intelligences that those people with high intelligence should rule. He argued the problem could be solved if those of superior intelligence devoted themselves to understanding the problems of the lower mental levels. They would "be elected the rulers of the realm and then will come perfect government—Aristocracy in Democracy." Historian Clarence J. Karier has pointed out how strongly elitist ideas were present in the writings of Edward L. Thorndike. Thorndike wrote, "... in the long run, it has paid the 'masses' to be ruled by intelligence.... It seems safe to predict that the world will get better treatment by trusting its fortunes to its 95- or 99-percentile intelligences than it would get by itself." Thorndike claimed that the "argument for democracy is not that it gives power to all men without distinction, but that it gives greater freedom for ability and character to attain power."

The dream of building a social structure based on measured intelligence depended on the assumption that there existed something called native intelligence. The writers of intelligence tests in the twentieth century have worked from that premise, but they have never clearly been able to define what they mean by intelligence. For example, in 1969 psychologist Arthur R. Jensen wrote an article in the *Harvard Educational Review* attacking the idea that compensatory education programs such as Head Start could produce any lasting effect on a child's IQ. Jensen maintained that environmental factors were not as important in determining intelligence as genetic factors were. After reviewing the literature on the nature or meaning of intelligence, Jensen admitted that intelligence "like electricity, is easier to measure than to define." He believed it did not matter if an adequate definition of intelligence existed, because the important thing was the measurement of outward behavior. "There is no point in arguing the question," Jensen wrote, "to which there is no answer, the question of what intelligence really is." The important thing in Jensen's mind was that through the relationship between certain kinds of measurable behavior one could gain some understanding of the phenomena.

It was just as true at the beginning of the century as it was in 1969 that no one was constructing intelligence tests around an adequate definition of intelligence. The pioneer work in test development was done in France by Alfred Binet, who, under the direction of the French Minister of Public Instruction, in 1904 developed a test for placing children into special schools. The concept of native intelligence used by Binet was both vague and relative. On the one hand Binet defined native intelligence as "judgment otherwise called good sense, initiative, the faculty of adapting one's self to circumstances." On the other hand, Binet stated that intelligence was relative to the social situation of an individual. Thus "an attorney's son who is reduced by his intelligence to the condition of a menial employee is a moron . . . likewise a peasant, normal in ordinary surroundings of the fields, may be considered a moron in the city." This relative social value given to intelligence is the key to understanding what Binet meant by native intelligence. Binet believed that measurement of intelligence only became important when society shifted from an agricultural base to one dependent on the corporate forms of social organization of the city and factory. The rustic surroundings of the rural village did not require the use of the type of intelligence needed in the urban and industrial world. For Binet successful living in the city and performance in the factory required the thing he called native intelligence, which was the ability to function in a socially efficient manner in a highly organized social structure.

One important thing to note about Binet is that his work was validated not in terms of a conception of intelligence, but in terms of a social criterion. This was to prove equally true of his American counterparts. Since there existed no adequate definition of intelligence, tests were validated by correlating them with other factors, such as social success and other tests. The nature of the intelligence measure was therefore directly related to the type of correlations the test constructor chose to make. For the early test writers the most common form of correlation was with some form of social success, such as academic success. This meant that the measurement of intelligence reflected the social values of the test constructor.

Building a social organization based on intellectual ability required the development of a group intelligence test. Individual tests such as the Binet were impractical to use with masses of people. The first major group intelligence test was developed in the United States for the army during World War I. As with other intelligence tests, these were validated in terms of social success. The criterion used in the army was ability to be a good soldier, which meant the ability to function well in a highly disciplined and highly stratified social organization. The writers of the army tests did not feel that this limited their applicability. In their minds the modern army represented an ideal form of social organization. Robert Yerkes, head of the U.S.

Army psychology team, wrote after the war, "Great will be our good fortune if the lesson in human engineering which the war has taught is carried over directly and effectively into our civil institutions and activities." The school, of course, was included in this dream of human engineering.

It is important to understand this fact about the World War I tests, because they became models for future group tests developed in this country. Two series of tests were developed during the war for the purpose of classifying army personnel. One was the Alpha test for literates, and the other was the Beta test for illiterates. After the armistice was signed, the government flooded the market with unused Alpha and Beta test booklets, which were immediately utilized by psychologists and educators. Guy M. Whipple, a leading psychologist of the time, reported in 1922 that the army Alpha tests were most widely used in colleges because they were the first group tests constructed by a team of well-known psychologists, they had been tested on large numbers of men in the army, and "the test blanks were procurable for several months after the armistice at prices far below what other tests could be produced. . . ."

The committee of psychologists who developed the army tests first met at H. H. Goddard's Vineland Institute in New Jersey on May 28, 1917. The committee had been organized by Robert M. Yerkes, who at the time was president of the American Psychological Association. Earlier in the year Yerkes had issued a newsletter announcing that he would appoint a committee of psychologists to gather "all useful information concerning the varied aspects of the actual and possible practical relations of psychology to military affairs. . . ." This group, consisting of Yerkes, M. V. Bingham, H. H. Goddard, T. H. Haines, L. M. Terman, F. L. Wells, and G. M. Whipple, decided at their first meeting at Vineland to confine the committee's work "chiefly to the classification of recruits on the basis of intellectual ability, with special reference to the elimination of the unfit and the identification of exceptionally superior ability."

This group of psychologists spent little time debating the

nature of the intelligence they were measuring. They were primarily interested in getting the job done as quickly as possible. Goddard admitted after the war, "We do not know what intelligence is." Working with amazing speed the group composed the tests between May 28, 1917 and June 10, 1917. They recessed for 2 weeks and met again on June 25 to revise the group examination method. On July 1 they received $2500 to test their examination in military camps. By July 7 they were able to send a copy of the examiner's guide to the printer.

Theoretical issues were set aside at Vineland because of the immense pressures felt because of the war. Yerkes wrote later, "Relatively early in this supreme struggle, it became clear to certain individuals that the proper utilization of man power, and more particularly of mind and brain power, would assure ultimate victory." The key idea for the war effort was the creation of a "military machine," a machine in which not only the implements of war had to have their proper place, but also one in which men were classified and utilized to their fullest extent. Originally the plan had been to use the intelligence tests to weed out the intellectually incapable, but as plans developed, they became the primary instruments for fitting men into the war machine. The tests provided the selective means for assuring that all parts of the machine worked effectively and smoothly. Native intelligence in this context meant the ability to function within the army. The tests were administered by a team of 100 officers and 800 enlisted men to almost 2 million members of the army. It was found that nearly 30 percent of the million and a half for whom statistics were available were unable to read and understand newspapers or write letters home and were given the special Beta test. Of those tested, close to 8000 were recommended for immediate discharge, 10,000 recommended for labor battalions or other service organizations, and over 9000 for development battalions for further observation and training.

The value of the Army tests depended on their ability to select good soldiers. In one army camp officers were asked to rate their men according to "practical soldier value." These ratings were compared to a soldier's test score, and there was found to be a high correlation between an officer's rating and the results of the Alpha and Beta tests. In validating the tests with officer's ratings in other army camps the coefficient of correlation was found to be between .50 and .70. Robert Yerkes concluded, "The results suggest that intelligence is likely to prove the most important single factor in determining a man's value to the military service."

What "practical soldier value" meant for army life was the ability to follow orders and function within a rigidly disciplined and highly organized institutional structure. The group examination instructions for the Alpha test provides ample evidence that this was the implied meaning of intelligence as used in the test. The instructions became the model for future examination booklets. For years after World War I students taking tests were subjected to the same type of instructions given soldiers during the war. The instructions began, "When everything is ready E. (examiner) proceeds as follows: 'Attention! The purpose of this examination is to see how well you can remember, think and carry out what you are told to do.... The aim is to help find out what you are best fitted to do in the Army.... Now in the army a man often has to listen to commands and carry them out exactly. I am going to give you some commands to see how well you can carry them out." In the schools this would often be translated into, "Part of being a good student is your ability to follow directions." What any former test taker will recognize were the instructions, "When I call 'Attention,' stop instantly whatever you are doing and hold your pencil up—so. Don't put your pencil down to the paper until I say 'Go.'... Listen carefully to what I say. Do just what you are told to do. As soon as you are through, pencils up. Remember, wait for the word 'Go.'"

Army test correlations with teacher ratings were very close to that of "practical soldier value." The army and the school, of course, represent similar forms of organization. The superintendent sits as commander of the armies, the principal acts as field commander, the teachers as officers, and below this command is a vast army of pupils. Orders flow from above, and pupils, like soldiers, receive privileges but are without rights. Both organizations handle large numbers of recruits, which requires discipline and obedience to instructions. Soldiers must loyally obey commands and students must have faith that the directions they receive are in their best interests. The reported correlations with teacher ratings were between .67 and .82. Interestingly, the correlations with officer ratings and teacher ratings were both higher than the .50 and .60 with school marks. If one assumes officer and teacher ratings depend more on character evaluation than grades, one could conclude that the group intelligence test was a test of the ability of the individual personality to adapt to organizational forms.

There was evidence given that suggested the group tests did discriminate against certain personality types. For tests such as Alpha and Beta, correlated with army life, and other tests correlated with ability in school, discrimination was against those who could not function well in highly organized institutional structures. If one assumes, and this assumption has not been disproven, that engineers represent a more organizationally directed type of personality than doctors, one result of the Alpha test lends support to this argument. Army psychologists during World War I had difficulty explaining the fact that engineering officers scored one grade higher on the test than medical officers. The head of the army psychology team admitted, "There is no obvious reason for assuming that the military duties of the engineer demand higher intelligence or more mental alertness than do those of the medical officer." The army psychologists tried to handle this result by arguing that there was an uneven distribution of intelligence among the various branches of the service. The point they might have missed was that medical men might have less "practical soldier" value than engineers which, after all, was what the group intelligence tests were supposed to measure.

The fact that the Alpha and Beta tests appeared to discriminate against certain personality types points out one of the major difficulties in defining and measuring native intelligence. Test constructors often work on the premise that there exists something called native intelligence, which is distinct from character, emotions, and learned behavior. Yet when tests of native intelligence are validated, it is always with something that requires the functioning of these other characteristics. Success in social conduct in the army and in the school certainly depend on character and control of emotions. Separating native intelligence from these factors is an extremely difficult and perhaps impossible task. If native intelligence as measured by the Alpha and Beta tests reflected ability to be a good soldier, the measurements most certainly included more than some isolated ingredient called native intelligence.

In general, test constructors were never able to clearly distinguish between native intelligence and character. Alfred Binet firmly believed native intelligence was independent of the ability to learn in school. Scholastic aptitude, he argued, required "attention, will and character; for example a certain docility, a regularity of habits, and especially continuity of effort." Yet he believed modern problems of social disorganization could be traced to a lack of native intelligence. This suggested that effective character required a high native intelligence. H. H. Goddard argued that the measurement of intelligence was an indication of how well an individual could control his emotions. This meant the level of intelligence indicated the type of character. The wise man was also the good man. Edward L. Thorndike went so far as to suggest that the ability to do well on tests gave evidence of justice and compassion. He tried to make his intelligence tests difficult and long so they would show not only an individual's intelligence but also "his ability to stick to a long and, at the end, somewhat distasteful task." A report was received from one institution of higher learning using the Thorndike test in the early 1920s that "two or three students fainted under the three-hour strain, and the faculty became indignant at this alleged imposition of hardship."

The difficulty psychologists were having defining intelligence and separating it from other character traits was made quite clear in a symposium conducted by the *Journal of Educational Psychology* shortly after the end of the war. The editors of the journal asked leading psychologists two questions: "(1) What (do you) conceive 'intelligence' to be, and by what means (can it) best be measured by group tests;" and, (2) What are the most crucial 'next steps' in research?" The responses were varied and confusing and most likely left the readers at that time without any clear indication of exactly what group intelligence tests were measuring. The most popular response to the meaning of intelligence was the ability to adapt to new situations. This was a Darwinian argument premised on the idea that the selective factor in human evolution was the functioning of the mind. Not only had William James defined mind in these terms in his *Principles of Psychology*, but Alfred Binet and the writers of the Alpha and Beta tests also had worked in this tradition. As a definition it added little clarity to the meaning of native intelligence. Was it a separate faculty, or did adaptation depend on the total character of the individual?

Lewis M. Terman, a former member of the Alpha and Beta group, tried to resolve the problem, but only added more confusion to the debate. Terman's fame was not only a product of his work on the army tests, but also of his Stanford revision of the Binet test and of his own group intelligence test. He was considered one of the leading authorities on test construction of his time. His contribution to the symposium consisted of two papers, one answering the questions and the other defending the Stanford-Binet tests. Terman attempted to define intelligence as the mental functions required to adapt to new problems and conditions of life. These mental functions involved the ability to form new concepts and understand their significance. "An individual," Terman wrote, "is intelligent in proportion as he is able to carry on abstract thinking." But he also stated "that social competency and educational possibilities both depend largely upon non-intellectual mental traits."

While he attempted to disavow any connection between character and intelligence as measured by tests, he did link social success with intelligence. Contradicting himself, he wrote, "It cannot be disputed, however, that in the long run it is the races which excel in abstract thinking that eat while others starve, survive epidemics, master new continents . . . substitute science for taboos and justice for revenge. The races which excel in conceptual thinking could, if they wished, quickly exterminate or enslave all the races notably their inferiors in this respect." Terman contradicted his position even further by suggesting that the leaders of any society were those whose intelligence dominated their behavior. Advancing an elitist idea about social control, one often found in the early testing movement, Terman argued, "any given society is ruled, led, or at least molded by the five or ten percent of its members whose behavior is governed by ideas."

Terman's ideas, of course, did not contradict the idea that intelligence was the best indicator of the value of a soldier to the army. Terman did suggest a much broader conception of intelligence as a measurement of social efficiency. Implied in Terman's discussion of gradations of intelligence was the idea that intelligence was linked to not only an organizational type of personality, but also to the ability to contribute to technological enterprises. Terman suggested that if a little intelligence were added to a pick and shovel worker, "he may be able to repair your automobile, build you a house according to an architect's specifications, or nurse you in illness." If a large measure of intelligence were added, he could "design a new type of engine, draft the plans for a skyscraper, or discover a curative serum." Terman's levels of intellectual advancement had nothing to do with ability to be just or compassionate, or with artistic ability. It is often difficult for people raised in the twentieth century to realize that in former times people were rated in terms of honor, justice, humility, and artistic creativity. Terman's standards were purely in terms of ability to solve technological and scientific problems.

This conception of intelligence fitted nicely into the social efficiency form of intelligence. Intelligence was an indication of the ability to function in modern corporate forms of activity, such as the army, the factory, and the school. It was also an indicator of what contribution the individual could make to the solution of the technical problems that arose in these complex organizations. The army Alpha and Beta tests functioned in this fashion. In the first place, the tests determined if you were intellectually capable of functioning within the organization of the army. The test results were then used to determine what contribution the individual could make to the technical problems of the army. If his scores were low, the soldier was given a pick and shovel. As Yerkes stated, intelligence was considered the most important single factor in determining a man's value to the army.

The army Alpha and Beta tests were, therefore, premised on a particular conception of the good society and a particular attitude toward the nature of intelligence. The army was considered an ideal form of social organization. The model, as Goddard suggested, was the beehive, where everyone performed a task suited to his capabilities. The group IQ test, by accomplishing this feat, was to advance society by assuring that no ounce of brain power was lost. Social discontent and problems were to dissolve with the proper classification of men. "A man who is doing work well within the capacity of his ability," Goddard wrote, "is apt to be very happy and contented and it is very difficult to disturb any such person by any kind of agitation." The nature of the intelligence to be measured was directly linked to the ideal of the good society. It was a measure of one's ability to function within this form of organization.

Group intelligence tests made it possible after World War I to classify large numbers of students in the public schools. The introduction of mass testing began what could be called the nature-nurture debates in education. The basic issue was whether nature of mental inheritance or the influences of environment and training were the primary determinants of success in schooling. At the heart of the debate was the other important issue of the nature of a democratic society. Mental tests suggested that not all men were equal or capable of being equal. Because of the social criteria used by test writers for validation of their tests, this inequality tended to follow class and color lines. The common argument for those who had faith in the reliability of intelligence tests was that the poor were poor because of low intelligence and that blacks had not significantly progressed in American society because their race was genetically inferior.

One example of the use of testing following the war was the program developed by the Detroit Public Schools. The head of the psychological clinic of the Detroit Schools reported in 1922 that prior to the war the clinic had concentrated on the use of individual tests to select backward children for special classes. After the war Detroit launched a massive testing program that led to the classification of 60 percent of the students into an average (Y) group, 20 percent into a backward (Z) group, and 20 percent into a superior (X) group. The director of this clinic commented in reporting his work, "The successful development of group tests of general intelligence in the United States Army in 1917 and 1918 and the adoption of the group method by hundreds of school systems is now an old story." The classification of children into different ability groups led to a differentiated program of studies. In a program that was fairly typical of the ones being implemented throughout the country, the Y group was given the existing course of study, the Z group a simplified version, and the X group an "enriched" course of study.

It was this type of widespread use of the group intelligence tests that sparked the nature-nurture debate. The major forum for the debate was the National Society for the Study of Education. The Society devoted their 1928 and 1940 yearbooks to the topic of intelligence and its nature and nurture. The influence of the writers of the army group intelligence tests was felt throughout the debate. Guy M. Whipple, a member of the original army testing committee, edited both of the yearbooks devoted to the nature-nurture controversy. Lewis M. Terman was chairman of the committee that gathered material for the 1928 yearbook and led the argument for the nature side of the debate in both the 1928 and 1940 yearbooks. In general the debate failed to resolve the issue of whether nature was more important than nurture, but during the course of the debate important beliefs about education were brought into question.

In 1928 Lewis M. Terman defined the importance of the debate in terms of the future goals of education. Terman argued, "If the differences found are due in the main to controllable factors of environment and training, then theoretically, at least, they can be wiped out by appropriate educational procedures—procedures which it would then become our duty to provide." This meant that if environmental factors were found to be the most important, the school could be utilized to create an equalitarian society. Much of the educational rhetoric of the nineteenth century that had supported the growth of public systems of education had been premised on the belief that men were perfectable and could be fundamentally changed within the school. If environment proved to play a minor role, Terman stated, "then the duty of the school is clearly to provide for differentiated training which will take these native differences into account."

The two most important studies between 1920 and 1940 that supported the role of nurture were conducted by a group of psychologists at the University of Chicago and at the Iowa Child Welfare Research Station. In 1928 the University of Chicago reported its lengthy study on the effect of foster homes on the intelligence of children. The Chicago study tested one group of children before they were placed in foster homes. It was found after they were retested that those in better foster homes gained considerably more in intelligence than did those in the poorer homes. Another comparison was made between siblings who had been reared in different foster homes. The correlation between their intelligence was found to be lower than that usually found for siblings raised together. The Chicago study also divided a group of siblings into two groups by putting into one group the member of each pair who was in the better foster home and into the other group the one in the poorer home. It was found that the mean IQ of the group in the poorer homes was 86, while those in the better homes was 95. The Chicago study also supported the nurture argument by showing that two unrelated children reared in the same home were found to resemble one another in intelligence.

The studies of the Iowa Child Welfare Research Station were reported in 1940. The original studies began in 1917 when the station was founded for the purpose of studying the relationship between the physical and mental development of school children. In 1921 a preschool laboratory was established in conjunction with the research station. The preschool laboratory gave members of the station an opportunity to test the effect of education on the level of intelligence. Children attending the preschool laboratory were given a Binet test in the fall and spring of each year. This provided an opportunity to compare results of the fall and spring tests, which covered the period of the child's attendance at the school, and to compare the spring test with that given in the fall of the following school year. This provided a sample of the child's development while both attending and not attending the laboratory school. The results of the studies showed that significant gains in IQ occurred during periods of preschool attendance and not during nonattendance. The Iowa studies also included the results of a preschool program conducted for 3 years in an orphanage. All available children in the orphanage were divided into a preschool and a nonpreschool group. It was reported that the group of orphans who did not attend the preschool program lost 16.2 IQ points, whereas those who attended the preschool gained 0.5 points.

While the Chicago and Iowa studies supported the belief in

the ameliorative ability of education, the majority of other studies between 1920 and 1940 cast serious doubts on the importance of education. For instance, a study was conducted in two New York public schools and reported in the 1928 yearbook of the National Society for the Study of Education. It concluded that there was no relationship between school attendance and intelligence or educational achievement. Students within the two schools were given the Stanford Revision of the Binet-Simon Intelligence scale and the Stanford Achievement Test to measure their all-round educational achievement. The attendance records of all the children were summarized to determine their actual number of days of attendance during their entire school career. The tests and the attendance records showed a great deal of variability among the students of the two schools. In terms of attendance, for instance, the range for eight-year olds was 499 days, that is, the difference between the highest number of days of attendance and the lowest. For thirteen-year olds the range of attendance was 1094 days. In correlating attendance with educational achievement it was found there was no significant relationship. The report stated, "Apparently, differences in the amount of schooling of these pupils of single age do not account for differences in their mental and their educational development." The only significant relationship the study could make was between intelligence and educational achievement. The conclusion was "that intelligence has contributed much more heavily than either attendance or age to the educational achievement of the children studied."

The New York study undercut all arguments for enforcing increased school attendance and lengthening the school year. What the study seemed to say was that educational achievement did not depend on schooling, but on individual intelligence. It did not matter how often a child went to school; if he was bright, he would learn anyway. Compulsory school laws and lengthened school years accomplished nothing in terms of

educational achievement. Their only purpose, this study seemed
to suggest, was to keep the children off the streets and out of
the labor market.

The 1928 yearbook also included another study that cast
doubts on the possibility of educational improvement. This
study reported there was no relationship between the money
spent on education and educational achievement. The study included 1796 students who had graduated from Iowa high
schools and had attended the State University of Iowa. Costs
were computed on the basis of how much each high school
district spent per pupil, and these were compared to a general
educational achievement examination given the students upon
graduation from high school and with their grades earned during their first semester at the university. The study concluded,
"Intelligence, as measured by the Thorndike test, is of far more
importance in determining the effectiveness of training than is
cost per pupil . . . the cost of public-school education seems not
to influence to any important extent attainment in institutions
of higher learning."

Other studies published under the auspices of the National
Society for the Study of Education also indicated that little
value could be gained by extending nursery school education.
Contrary to the Iowa preschool studies, a study conducted at
the Lincoln School of Teachers College at Columbia University
found there was no real difference in intelligence quotients
when the results of testing before school experience and after
a period of schooling were compared. A study of young children at the University of Minnesota found that there was an
increase of IQ for both those who did and did not attend
nursery school, but that there was practically "a zero correlation . . . found between gain in I.Q. and length of nursery-school
attendance."

On the surface one might have concluded that there was
little reason for those who supported the nature side of the
debate to support extended schooling. This was a problem
Terman tried to tackle at the 1928 Boston meeting of the Na-

tional Society for the Study of Education. Terman argued that the acceptance of the idea that intelligence test scores are not influenced by schooling did not mean the rejection of mass education nor "that we might as well discard our alphabet, nail up our schools, and retreat to the jungle." The question, he believed, was not whether the school should be abandoned, but what form education should take. To Terman, studies between the relationship of schooling and intelligence and educational achievement suggested that the schools placed too much emphasis on the mastery of subjects. Mastery of subjects did not depend on length of schooling, costs, or other factors, but on a factor that was independent of schooling: intelligence. The school viewed in this context, he argued, should "place more emphasis than we now do upon the ethical and social ends of education, and care more than we now do about making the school a wholesome place to live."

Support for either side of the debate depended on which set of studies one wished to consider important. Educational leader Charles H. Judd reacted very negatively to Terman's comments at the Boston meeting. Judd told the gathered members of the society, "There are many of us who have felt ... there is a demand in America for the best possible environment for every child and we have watched with some anxiety the spread of what appeared to be a fatalistic theory among those who have adopted without reservations the view that the I.Q. never changes." He singled out the Chicago study of children placed in foster homes as giving proof that IQ was not a constant factor. Terman earlier in the meeting had stated about the Chicago study: "I do not find their data conclusive." In fact, Judd completely disagreed with the interpretation given by Terman to most of the studies published by the society. Judd argued that they "ought to put an end to the superficial fatalism that has been rampant in certain quarters and ought to turn educational science into an experimental endeavor to discover how to transmit social inheritances as readily and as completely as possible to all people."

The fatalism that concerned Judd was exactly what crept into those quarters committed to the concept of native intelligence. The nature of the fatalism was directly related to the role intelligence tests were playing in the schools. The school could not eliminate differences between individuals, but it could properly classify according to their future social positions. The fact that classification paralleled class and racial lines did not bother the writers of intelligence tests. They believed this only added further proof to the validity of their tests. When Alfred Binet was confronted with the fact that his measurement of native intelligence varied with social class, his response was, "That this difference exists one might suspect because our personal investigations, as well as those of many others, have demonstrated that children of the poorer class are shorter, weigh less, have smaller heads and slighter muscular force, than a child of the upper class; they less often reach the high school; they are more often behind in their studies."

The same feeling that social class differences resulted from differences in levels of intelligence also entered discussions of racial differences. Following World War I Carl C. Brigham, an Assistant Professor of Psychology at Princeton University, analyzed the results of the Alpha and Beta tests in terms of their implications for racial differences. His book, *A Study of American Intelligence,* contained a foreword by the head of the army psychology team, Robert M. Yerkes, in which Yerkes praised Brigham's study as "substantial as to fact and important in its practical implications." Brigham's major thesis was that average level of intelligence in the United States had been declining with the steady immigration of inferior racial stock. He divided the racial stock of America into Nordic, Alpine, Mediterranean, and Negro. According to his classification, Nordic stock originated in countries such as Sweden, Norway, and England, Alpine stock from countries such as Romania and Austria-Hungary, and Mediterranean blood from areas such as Italy, Greece, and Spain. Brigham's analysis of Alpha and Beta tests showed Nordic groups in America superior to the Mediterranean, and placed Negroes at the bottom of the scale. Quoting Madison Grant's *The Passing of the Great*, Nordics were described as "domineering, individualistic, self-reliant, and jealous of their personal freedom both in political and religious systems, and as a result they are usually Protestants." It was Brigham's contention that with increased immigration to the United States of Alpine and Mediterranean groups, the influence of superior Nordic blood on the racial stock of America was declining.

Racial analysis of this type contained not only the social values inherent in the intelligence tests, but also the social values of the interpreter. One of the striking results of the Alpha and Beta tests was the fact that Northern Negroes exhibited a higher intelligence level than Southern Negroes. One might have assumed from this result that environment played an important role in determining the score on intelligence tests. Some writers did contend the results reflected the superior educational opportunities of the Northern states. Brigham, on the other hand, argued that the differences could be attributed to differences of native intelligence. Since Southern and Northern Negroes of equal schooling showed striking differences in intelligence, Brigham inferred that the Northern Negro was probably superior to the Southern Negro. This, he stated, was true of any race. Some members of the race with higher levels of intelligence would be able to adapt to new and complex situations. Those who are unable to adapt, namely Southern Negroes and lower-class whites, reflect inferior hereditary endowment.

Differences in levels of intelligence among racial groups became one of the common findings of intelligence studies. These results, of course, reflected the social criteria used to validate the tests. For instance, the 1928 yearbook of the National Society for the Study of Education contained a study conducted at the George Peabody College for Teachers where white children were shown to be superior to Negro children in learning ability. The introduction to the study written by the editors of the society stated, "Differences between white and Negro children upon this test are found to be comparable to differences repeatedly found in previous studies. . . . This carries the implication . . . that the differences between white and Negro subjects . . . are due to a more elemental difference than can be produced by mere differences in educational opportunities." This editorial statement reflected Brigham's feeling that "The average Negro child can not advance through an educational curriculum adapted to the Anglo-Saxon child in step with that child. To select children of equal education, age for age, in the two groups, is to sample either superior Negroes or inferior whites."

The fatalistic idea of poverty and racial differences as resulting from inferior genetic factors shifted the argument for social reform from education to eugenics. Since education could not eliminate inherited differences, the only hope for social reform for those committed to the concept of native intelligence was a program of selective breeding. In 1914 H. H. Goddard argued, in a study entitled *Feeble-Mindedness: Its Causes and Consequences*, that crime, pauperism, intemperance, and prostitution resulted from insufficient levels of intelligence existing in a complex modern urban and industrial society. He believed low levels of intelligence were adequate for functioning in the simple agricultural societies of the past, but not for modern society. For people like Goddard the only solution was a program of eugenics that restricted the breeding of those with lower forms of intelligence. E. L. Thorndike, in his last major work published in 1940, contended the solution for the population problem was not restrictive breeding but planned breeding. Thorndike claimed that a program of eugenics would increase the quality of the population, which would, in turn, increase productivity to sustain a greater population.

While the testing movement never created a national eugenics program, it did result in the schools defining as one of their important functions the selection and classification of students. In an article in the Fall 1959 issue of the *Harvard Educational Review*, sociologist Talcott Parsons divided the socialization functions of the modern school into two components—"commitment to the implementation of broad *values* of society, and commitment to the performance of a specific type of role within the *structure* of society. . . ." Indoctrination into the values of society had been one of the major arguments for public systems of education in the nineteenth century and represented a traditional educational concern. Selecting and committing students to a specific social role in society became one of the major social purposes of the school in the twentieth century.

During the 1950s and 1960s the classification function of the school came under serious criticism from groups attempting to use education as a vehicle for social reform. The civil rights movement and poverty programs resurrected the dream of the school as a major instrument for social reform. The reform spirit ran counter to the argument of the testing movement that little could be accomplished through education to eradicate social and racial barriers. One of the major targets of the new reform spirit was the classification of students. The early testing movement had readily accepted the forms of classification that placed most lower-class students into vocational tracks and most upper-class students into college preparatory classes. To the original writers of intelligence tests this represented the facts of life. The poor were poor because of deficient native intelligence. The new breed of reformer did not accept this argument and saw the selective mechanisms of the school as a form of social condemnation.

One of the major studies of the early 1960s that showed how the differentiation of students was paralleling social class lines was a study of the Detroit school system, *Education and Income* by Patricia Sexton. As noted earlier, Detroit began differentiating students immediately after World War I when group intelligence tests became available. Sexton divided the Detroit school population into groups according to family income. She compared family income to achievement scores and IQ scores. The IQ tests were the major means for segregating students within the school system. According to her study the average IQ increased with higher levels of family income. The Detroit schools used an intelligence scale of from one to six. Sexton's calculations showed the lowest income level ($3000– 5000) having an intelligence score of 2.79, the next income level ($5000–7000) a score of 3.31, the following income group ($7000– 9000) an average of 4.55, and the highest income bracket ($9000–) an average of 5.09.

Numerous studies similar to Sexton's were used during the 1950s and 1960s to discredit intelligence tests as being socially biased. Such attacks were not unfounded nor would they necessarily have been rejected by the original developers of the tests. The tests were socially biased from the very beginning, both in terms of the way they were validated and in terms of the vision the test constructor had of the good society. Any measurement of human abilities requires some socially defined standard. If society decides the quality of being humane is what distinguishes intelligence, that will be built into the test. All a science of psychology can do is to determine the best means of measurement. What is to be measured is up to society and the social values of the psychologist.

The most important attack on the intelligence test came indirectly from segments of the youth culture movement during the late 1960s. This was an attack that focused on the type of society the intelligence testing movement hoped to create. The ideal of an efficient society that properly classified students in school and channeled them into suitable social roles proved repugnant to members of the youth movement. Part of this reaction was caused by extension of the draft during the Viet Nam War. There was a growing feeling against the total institutionalization of American life. The adolescent in the United States found himself with the limited choice of either continued schooling, the army, or a job classified as being in the national interest. In 1965 *Ramparts* magazine published a document called "Channeling," which had been part of a selective service orientation kit. The document touched off a flurry of concern about the meaning of democracy in a society that attempted to channel people into proper social roles either through schooling or the selective service. The document claimed as one of the functions of selective service the channeling of manpower into activities considered to be in the national interest. "The psychology of granting wide choice under pressure to take action," the document stated, "is the American or indirect way of achieving what is done by direction in foreign countries where choice is not permitted."

Many of the youth of the late 1960s came to view the schools merely as custodial institutions designed to fit the individual into a social slot. Yippie leader Jerry Rubin claimed in *Do It!* in 1970, "The function of school is to keep white middle class youth off the streets." The message society was giving youth according to Rubin was ". . . history is over, fit in." It was exactly this fitting in that youth was tending to rebel against. Institutional channeling was removing all meaning and importance from individual life-styles. The efficient functioning of a society seemed to mean the suppression of the individual for the efficiency of the social organization. Rubin warned, "A society which suppresses adventure makes the only adventure the suppression of that society."

Other strands of popular culture also joined the attack against the concept of a good society being the result of the efficient allocation of manpower resources. In the 1950s Kurt Vonnegut, Jr. wrote a satirical novel about a society entirely organized around a computerized testing program. The book, *Player Piano*, depicted a superefficient machine society where only those with high intelligence ratings found meaningful employment in running the machines. Because of the efficiency of the machines and social organization, meaningless work had to be created for the majority of the society. During the course of the novel, a secret organization called the Ghost Shirt Society was formed and attempted to overthrow the system. One of the statements issued by the Ghost Shirt Society summed up the growing concern in America about the direction of its social organization. The letter from the society stated, "Without regard for the changes in human life patterns that may result, new machines, new forms of organization, new ways of increasing efficiency, are constantly being introduced. To do this without regard for the effects on life patterns is lawlessness." The members of the Ghost Shirt Society believed "that there must be virtue in inefficiency, for Man is inefficient. . . ."

chapter four

youth and the custodial role of the schools

$t$he 1960s witnessed the rise of an important youth movement and a rebellion against the custodial role of the schools. Both these phenomena were related to the rise of technology and to urbanization, which reduced the economic usefulness of youth and eliminated for it any immediate important function in the social structure. During the course of the twentieth century the school assumed more and more the role of guardianship over what was to become a new social group. As youth became segregated from the rest of society, it developed its own set of social standards and tastes. This was the result of institutionalization in the school and exploitation by the commercial market. As youth lost its importance as a producer, its role as a consumer increased until it was defined as a special market for goods and services. But by the 1960s youth was no longer satisfied with its essentially useless colonial status and began to define for itself a new social role as crusader against national and international injustices.

The story of the development of the custodial role of the school and youth culture begins in the United States in the late nineteenth century as part of the response to post-Civil War urban and industrial changes. The custodial function of the school was the result of an antiurban attitude and rural bias that sought to protect the child from the rapidly expanding urban culture at the beginning of the century and the growing recognition that youth was without a meaningful and functional social and economic role. These two primary factors increased the importance of schooling in American life and expanded the protective role of the school.

In 1947 at the age of eighty Caroline Pratt sat down to write the story of her adventures as founder and director of the City and Country School in New York City. Her life had spanned almost a century of change, from a predominantly rural to an urban America. Born in Fayetteville, New York in 1867, she wrote that during her childhood "school was not very important to children who could roam the real world freely for their learning." She belonged to a generation that witnessed the parallel rise of the importance of the city and the school in American life. It was a generation that continually reminisced wistfully from the perspective of city life about the wonderful world of country living, and a generation that exhibited an underlying hostility and antagonism toward urban life. Caroline Pratt believed the school had become essential in the modern world because the urban child could no longer understand his world by himself. "This is the change I have seen," she wrote, "from a world in which children could learn as they grew in it, to a world so far beyond the grasp of children, that only the school can present it to them in terms which they can understand. . . ."

The rural bias of city dwellers at the beginning of the century was indicative of the nature of urban growth in the United States. After the Civil War the urban population grew mainly as a result of migration from rural areas of the United States and Europe. Census data from 1900–1910 showed that only 21.6 percent of the 11,826,000 increase in city population in the United States was the result of natural increase. The rest of the increase, besides a small gain from cities expanding their borders, was from immigration from Europe and native rural to urban migration. Most of the European immigrants who settled in American cities had been rural dwellers. The growth of cities in this context meant that attitudes toward the city were heavily latent with traditional rural distrust of the city. Added to this rural distrust was an antiimmigrant feeling prevalent among native Americans. The school was viewed as a protective shield between the child and the urban environment and as a means of protecting American values by Americanizing the immigrant from Europe.

Combined with the rural bias was the realization that the child in the modern world lacked a functional social role. Caroline Pratt wrote that before urban living, "We did not merely stand by while the work of our simpler world was done; I drove the wagon in haying.... At ten, my great-aunt used to say, I could turn a team of horses and a wagon in less space than a grown man needed to do it." John Dewey, in his famous "School and Society" lectures in 1899, stressed that in the small communities of the past children engaged in activities that were useful for the maintenance of the community. The farmer's son performed essential tasks on the farm, the son of the small craftsman contributed to the work of his father, and all the children helped to maintain the household. Modern industrialization and urbanization destroyed the usefulness of the child to the general workings of the family and community. Dewey believed this had important consequences for the education of children. It was through the performance of these tasks, Dewey believed, that the child had gained "training in habits of order and of industry, and in the idea of responsibility, of obligation to produce something in the world."

Children and adolescents did have an economic role in the early stages of industrialism. They were useful in performing repetitive tasks on the assembly line in the factory and provided an inexpensive source of labor. The campaign against child labor was a blend of humanitarianism and the expression from labor unions of a desire to remove what they considered the unfair competition of child labor. This campaign resulted in the passage of child labor laws and the extension of compulsory education that effectively closed the door on the possibility of youth having any functional economic role in the modern urban and industrial society. The informal usefulness of children in the household was curtailed by the very organization and specialization of the city. Heat, water, and waste removal became functions of the various departments of the city government. Most products used in the home were bought at the local store. In the more rural settings the child might have chopped and gathered wood for heating and cooking, helped the mother make candles and soap, or engaged in the many occupations that were later taken over by urban organizations. The child's informal functions in the city were reduced to trivial activities, such as going to the store for items the mother forgot or preparing the trash for collection.

The important point was that in terms of modern urban culture, youth was useless. During the early part of the twentieth century the realization of the social uselessness of the child was combined with a feeling that the city did not provide a proper environmental setting for childhood development. Cramped streets filled with the disorder of city traffic provided little opportunity for the free activities of childhood play. The street corner life of adolescents often led to various forms of juvenile delinquency. It was believed by many during this period that the bright lights and commercialization of the city streets were leading children down the path of moral corruption. Even as early as 1805 the leader of the New York Free School Society was warning, "Great cities are, at all times, the nurseries and hot-beds of crimes. . . . And the dreadful examples of vice which are presented to youth, and the alluring forms in which it is arrayed . . . cannot fail of augmenting the mass of moral depravity."

Added to the belief in the moral corruption of the city was a romantic pastoralism that dominated a great deal of the discussion about urban education in the early part of the twentieth century. Americans had a long tradition of believing that contact with natural surroundings stimulated moral vitality and healthy living. G. Stanley Hall, the leader of the child study movement in the late nineteenth and early twentieth centuries, was appalled when a survey of "the contents of children's minds" in Boston showed how little the city child knew about country living. Hall was not only concerned about the deficiency in knowledge, but also about the effect on the total development of the child. He argued that the city child's lack of contact with the country caused both moral and mental retardation. The country child, Hall believed, because of his contact with nature, was mentally superior to the city child. Hall's concern found wider expression in the movement for "Fresh Air Funds." In large cities throughout the country money was provided usually through newspaper campaigns to send poor urban children to rural summer camps. It was believed that many of the problems of slum dwellers could be cured if the next generation were morally rejuvenated through exposure to country life.

The development of summer schools reflected the concern about the nonfunctional role of youth and the moral corruption of city living. One of the earliest proposals for a summer school was directed at the problem that there was nothing for children to do when not attending school during the summer. In 1872 the Cambridge School Committee argued for a summer school because summer was "a time of idleness, often of crime, with many who are left to roam the streets, with no friendly hand to guide them, save that of the police." Fifteen years later the superintendent of the same school district was still asking for a summer school in terms of it occupying unfilled time. He wrote in a school report in 1897, "The value of these schools consists not so much in what shall be learned during the few weeks they are in session as in the fact that no boy or girl shall be left with unoccupied time. Idleness is an opportunity for evil-doing ... these schools will cost money. Reform schools also cost money. ..."

The curriculum of some of the early summer schools was

heavily laden with a concern about exposing the child to the rehabilitating effects of nature. By the 1890s summer school programs had been established in most major cities, with Chicago developing one of the model programs. The nature study program of the Chicago summer schools included excursions into the country. This idea had widespread appeal. Jacob Riis, the famous writer on New York tenements, wrote in 1900 that New York schools "took a hint from Chicago" and took the children into the country. The principal of one of the Chicago summer schools described how when the first group of slum children got off the railroad at the end of the line, they crawled on their hands and knees to feel the country soil for the first time. It was pathetic, he wrote, "to see the children rush for the ill smelling and dusty chickweed of the roadside."

The same attitudes that shaped the development of summer schools influenced the establishment of city parks and playgrounds. During the 1880s and 1890s there was a widespread movement in most major urban areas in the United States to provide play areas for children and recreation centers for the urban adult. Originally the play movement tended to develop independently of the urban school until it was discovered the school area was a convenient place for playgrounds and that teachers could be used as playground directors after school hours. The highpoint of the whole movement was the development of an elaborate park system in Chicago in 1905 and the establishment in 1906 of the Playground and Recreation Association with Theodore Roosevelt and Jacob Riis as honorary President and Vice-President, respectively. The tone of the movement was that parks would end crime in the city and provide moral salvation for the child. A report of the Committee on Small Parks in New York City claimed, "Crime in our large cities is to a great extent simply a question of athletics." When a park was established in Mulberry Bend in New York City in the 1890s, Jacob Riis wrote that the area was made relatively free of crime because "the light has come in and made crime hideous. It is being let in wherever the slum has bred murder and robbery, bred the gang, in the past." In 1917 Henry S. Curtis, one of the key organizers of the Playground and Recreation Association and one of the leaders of the early playground movement, wrote that the major concern of the leaders of the play movement was that there was "little for the children to do in the cities, and that in this time of idleness the devil has found much for idle hands to do.... The home seems to be disappearing, and crime, despite an increasingly effective police and probation system, is increasing everywhere."

Besides summer school and the playground, the urban school was called on to occupy the city child's time in other ways. Early urban educators viewed one of their most important jobs as saving the city child from contact with an immoral environment. This attitude turned the school into a custodial institution that sought to institutionalize as much of the city child's life as possible. The expansion of extracurricular activities at the turn of the century was largely the result of the feeling that the child had nothing to do in the city but get into trouble. After-school clubs, dances, organized athletic events, and other forms of planned recreation were all designed to control the after-school life of the urban child. Paralleling the rise of extracurricular school activities was the development of other groups, such as the Boy Scouts, Girl Scouts, Campfire Girls, YMCA, YWCA, and various community-sponsored recreation clubs. The prevailing feeling was that a life of crime began in the unsupervised activities of the city streets.

The argument for expanding the custodial role of the urban school received support from psychological and sociological theories about the causes of juvenile delinquency. In 1912 J. Adams Puffer wrote *The Boy And His Gang*, which was to become a popular book on boy's gangs based on case histories the author had collected as principal of the Lyman School for Boys in Boston in the early 1900s. Puffer's book was written under the direction of G. Stanley Hall and reflected many of Hall's favorite theories. Hall believed that each stage of individual development matched a stage of the growth of civilization.

Growth in childhood, the years between four and eight, corresponded to a cultural epoch when hunting and fishing were the main activities of man. From eight to twelve the child recapitulated the humdrum life of savagery. Hall, as Rousseau did over 100 years before, believed the flood of passions beginning in puberty developed the social man. "The social instincts," he wrote, "undergo sudden unfoldment and the new life of love awakens." In terms of Hall's theory, adolescence corresponded to a period when civilization was in a turbulent stage of development. Hall believed city life was crushing this natural development and, more important, was misdirecting the developing social instincts of adolescence. To Hall the whole future of civilization depended on how the social instincts of youth were directed and utilized. He recommended for modern youth the organization of boys' clubs under the guidance of adults. These social organizations were to utilize the natural instincts of youth and "so direct intelligence and will as to secure the largest measure of social service, advance altruism and reduce selfishness, and thus advance the higher cosmic order."

Puffer wove these theories of Hall's through his own analysis of juvenile gangs. Puffer defined the gang age as being between ten and sixteen, and as corresponding to a tribal period in the development of man that "began somewhere this side of the glacial period, and came to an end with, let us say, the early middle ages." Puffer, like Hall, considered this period to be one of developing social instincts. The problem of gang crime, as Puffer saw it, was that cultural evolution had outdistanced biological evolution. Therefore apparent antisocial gang activities resulted from archaic racial instincts. Puffer noted that most crime committed by gangs centered around the stealing of food items. The stealing of pears, cakes, and bananas was the result of tribal predatory instincts. The solution to these problems, Puffer argued, was not to disband the gang, but to channel gang instincts into clubs and the boy scouts. Puffer believed that the cultivation of these social instincts was necessary for the development of a cooperative society. The gang, Puffer wrote, "is the earliest manifestation in man of that strange group-forming instinct, without which beehive and ant hill and human society would be alike impossible."

The courts and the schools picked up the language of gang behavior and often referred to juvenile delinquency as misdirected social instincts. An investigation of juvenile crime in Chicago published in 1912 argued that many youths brought into court were not really criminals, but had gotten into trouble because of natural, mischievous gang activities. The report stated that the charges that brought youth into court "often indicate social effort, misdirected unfortunately, but still social." The report went on to argue that the "gang, which is frequently responsible for the offences of its members, presents a social phenomenon of hopeful significance and promise when once understood and utilized." In the schools the work of after-school clubs and athletics were directed at capturing and properly developing the social instincts of youth. The urban school and community directed their efforts at turning juvenile gangs into healthy social groups.

During the 1920s America's leading school of urban sociology, under the direction of Robert Park at the University of Chicago, studied urban gangs and arrived at similar conclusions from the perspective of sociology. The sociologists at the University of Chicago rejected G. Stanley Hall's instinct theory of recapitulation and tried to explain juvenile delinquency in terms of the social conditions of the city. Their approach to the city was less antagonistic than previous American writers. They saw the great cultural advantages made available by a large concentration of population. The problem was not that the city itself bred immorality, but that social conditions in particular parts of the city led an individual to a life of crime. Their analysis of the social conditions of the city and the recognition that youth lacked a functional social role led them down the same path of thinking as previous writers. The problems of urban youth could not be solved until planned activities by the school, clubs, and community organizations occupied most of the after-school time of the child.

The major work on juvenile delinquency to emerge from the studies of the Chicago School was Fredric M. Thrasher's *The Gang*, published in 1927. Thrasher's study located 1313 gangs in the Chicago area. Not all of these gangs were involved in acts of delinquency, but those that were he found located in areas characterized by rapid change and shifting populations. These unstable conditions, he argued, undermined the traditional means of controlling and integrating youth into the social patterns of the community. Within the disorganized life of the slum area the family's traditional role of control over the child rapidly deteriorated. Religion and education had failed to maintain their importance in the life of the slum child because of outdated techniques and ideology. Both had also, according to Thrasher, neglected to provide adequate leisure-time activities. This failure was the most important contributor to juvenile ganging. The gang filled the void left by the disorganization of other social institutions in the urban environment. Youth, Thrasher argued, needed some institutional structure through which it could develop its personality and learn habits of good social action. The urban gang merely filled a need created by the disorganization of city life. What Thrasher prescribed as a remedy was joint community action in planning and regulating the activities of urban youth. "The common assumption," Thrasher wrote, "that the problem of boy delinquency will be solved by the multiplication of playgrounds and social centers in gang areas is entirely erroneous." Acting independently these institutions would fail to capture the majority of the children. The solution was introducing a leader who would coordinate all of these activities. Thrasher wrote, "The real problem is one of developing in these areas or introducing into them leaders who can organize the play of the boys, direct it into wholesome channels, and give it social significance."

Thrasher's argument broadened the scope of thinking about juvenile problems, but did not fundamentally alter the approach. The problem was still to occupy the city child's time with "wholesome" social activities. What the school, YMCA, and clubs had been trying to achieve independently, Thrasher was now suggesting had to be accomplished cooperatively. His hope was to transform the gang into some other form of organization. One example he cited was of a young Chicago gang called the "Holy Terrors" who regularly attacked a local factory with rocks and other vandalism. The president of the company solved the problem by inviting a local scout master to try and gain leadership of the gang. The scout master made friends with the gang members and eventually had them transformed into a Boy Scout Troop. This was the type of gang transformation Thrasher wanted accomplished on a community-wide basis. He quoted figures showing that Boys' Clubs in New York had not been an important factor in delinquency prevention during the period studied. The reason was the inability to reach the majority of children in the area around the Boys' Clubs because of a lack of general community planning that would evaluate the needs of the local youth population and develop strategies for bringing them into the clubs.

Thrasher's approach to juvenile delinquency placed the urban school in the total framework of community planning. This was one of the important effects of the rise of urban America on the schools. Because of the complexity of urban living, it was believed the schools could not accomplish their goals alone. There was great faith during the early part of the twentieth century that sociology would be able to rationalize the apparent chaos of city life. This attempted rationalization gave greater scope and meaning to the role of the school in society. Earlier educational leaders in the nineteenth century had defined broad goals for the school, such as creating a common political ideology, ending social class strife, and eliminating crime and poverty. But the role of the school was given even greater importance in the rising urban world of the twentieth century. It was believed that the city was causing the disintegration of the family and the community. It was the school that was asked to replace these institutions.

The family and the community were not, in fact, disintegrating, but were undergoing profound changes. Both the family and community are products of social organization and are constantly in a state of transition as social conditions change. Industrialization and urbanization did not destroy the family, but changed its form of organization. In terms of sociological theory made popular by sociologist Edward Ross in the late 1890s, the family and community were an important source of social control. Ross had defined two types of social control: external, that is, pressure applied directly by the police and government to maintain social order, and internal, that is, habits learned through the family, community, or school that made men act in an orderly fashion. Ross believed some form of social control was necessary in any society to assure its orderly functioning. Sociologists and educators immediately used the term social control to define the purpose of schooling. Throughout the early part of the twentieth century it was common for educators to speak of the decline of the family and community as meaning the need for increased social control through the schools.

The social control argument lent further support to the increasing custodial function of the school. It was argued that the communities of rural and small-town America were important factors of social control, because through close face-to-face relationships and the integrated economic life the child was given a sense of responsibility and taught the morals and customs of the group. The close working family of the small community played an even more important part in preparing the child to conduct himself according to the needs of social order. The city, it was believed, destroyed close face-to-face relationships and a sense of collective responsibility. City dwellers gained a sense of alienation and irresponsibility about the needs of their neighbors. City children were without the integrated social role they had in the small communities of the past. There was nothing called the community in the city to which they belonged and could learn proper social habits and attitudes. The family in the city underwent similar changes.

The family was no longer an integrated social unit. The child was without any important social role in the family and, because of the conditions of the city, the family could not adequately supervise the child's conduct. In terms of social control ideology, the school and other institutions had to replace these institutions. Robert Park wrote in the 1920s that organizations like the YMCA, Boy Scouts, youth clubs, and playground associations "have taken over to some extent the work which neither the home, the neighborhood, nor the other older communal institutions were able to carry on adequately." Park further argued, "It is around the public school and its solicitude for the moral and physical welfare of the children that something like a new neighborhood and community spirit tends to get itself organized."

The attempt to replace the social control of the family and community with the school was approached on two different levels. The school, by adopting a custodial function and assuming responsibility for an increasing share of the child's time, actually did relieve the family of many of the duties of educating their children. Whether it replaced the family in importance in shaping the child's behavior and future social conduct is a moot point. What we do know is that many educators thought and planned in these terms. One of the most extreme ideas along these lines came from sociologist Edward Ross. Ross not only argued that the family was losing its importance under the pressures of modernity, but also that it might be a good idea for the school to replace the family. Writing in his book on *Social Control*, he claimed, "Copy the child will, and the advantage of giving him his teacher instead of his father to imitate, is that the former is a picked person, while the latter is not."

The New Condition of Youth

The custodial and social control aspect of schooling took on added importance during the 1920s with the rapid increase of man-hour productivity. The ability of large numbers of the population to attend school always depends on the ability of the rest of the society to support those in school and out of production. A large majority attending school meant that workers in agriculture and manufacturing had to be highly productive and efficient. The amount of output per man-hour of work had been steadily increasing in the United States from the time of the Civil War. This was the result of advances in technology and more efficient forms of corporate organization. Between 1900 and 1910 output per man-hour increased by 14 percent and further increased between 1910 and 1920 by 21 percent. During the period of rapid economic growth in the 1920s productivity in terms of man-hours jumped another 27 percent.

The increase in productivity resulted in fewer youths involved in production, an increase in school enrollments, and the beginning of a youth culture. In 1900 62 percent of the male population from the ages of fourteen to nineteen were participating in the labor force. Between 1900 and 1920 the number dropped to 51.5 percent. During the 1920s the drop to 40.1 percent almost equaled that of the previous 20 years. The decline in participation of those between the ages of twenty and twenty-four was less dramatic than the younger group. In 1900 90.6 percent participated in the labor force, and by the end of the 1920s it was down to 88.8 percent. The decrease in participation in the labor force was reflected in increased school attendance. The most important and significant changes came during the 1920s. Between 1900 and 1920 school attendance for those between the ages of five and seventeen increased from 78.7 to 83.9 percent or an increase of 5.2 percent. For the 6-year period between 1920 and 1926 the percentage jumped another 6.5 percent to 90.4. College enrollment for those between the ages of eighteen and twenty-one followed the same pattern. In 1900 4 percent of the eighteen to twenty-one-year-old group was in college; by 1920 this was 8.1 percent. During the 1920s an increase of 4.3 percent in college enrollment more than equaled that of the previous 20 years.

The increase in productivity, affluence, and increased school attendance all contributed to making what has been called the flapper era or jazz age. The 1920s saw the beginning of a major generational split that manifested itself in the development of a youth culture. Of course, every era has felt a gap between the thinking and actions of its younger and older members. What was unique about the 1920s was that this gap manifested itself as a different life style. Large numbers of youth who were brought up in comparative affluence, free of concerns about involvement in production, began to develop a different style of life around the new technology of the twentieth century. The numbers involved might not have been as large as those in the later 1960s, but they were large enough to give members of the older generation the feeling there was a significant youth problem.

Youth of the 1920s developed a faddish style around the consumption of the new products of technology. The automobile of the 1920s gave youth a freedom that had not existed for previous generations. Those concerned with the youth problem traced the decline of morality, the free spirit, and rebellion against authority to the automobile. Lengthy articles and discussions appeared in popular magazines, such as *Survey*, on the automobile and morality. Combined with the automobile was the increasing accessibility of movie houses, different styles of clothing, dance, and later in the 1920s, the gin mills of prohibition. These conditions led a headmaster to lament before a Rotary Club in Trenton, New Jersey in 1926 about the maelstrom his students would be entering. When he was eighteen, he said, life was less difficult because there was no "prohibition," "ubiquitous automobile," "cheap theater," "absence of parental control," or "emancipation of womanhood."

Many Americans agreed with the headmaster at Lawrenceville that flapper dress, manners, and morals were leading youth straight down the path to hell. In 1923 the *Literary Digest* conducted a national survey asking high school principles, college presidents, college deans, the editors of college newspapers, and the editors of religious weeklies if they thought the younger generation was in peril. For those who wrote a case against the younger generation, the problem was increasing immorality. The editor of the *Moody Bible Institute Monthly* responded to the survey with the declaration that in both manners and morals, society "is undergoing not a revolution, but a devolution. That is to say, I am not so imprest by its suddenness or totalness as by its steady, uninterrupted degeneration." From a college newspaper editor came the opinion that "the modern dance has done much to break down standards of morals." Describing life at the University of Pennsylvania the editor complained, "To the girl of to-day petting parties, cigaretsmoking, and in many cases drinking, are accepted parts of existence.... She dresses in the lightest and most flimsy of fabrics. Her dancing is often of the most passionate nature...." A writer from the Phi Kappa Psi House in Evanston, Illinois summed up the general mood of the survey with, "One outstanding reflection on the young set to-day is the reckless pursuit of pleasure."

Youth culture of the 1920s tended to avoid involvement in social issues. A writer in a 1922 *New Republic* wishfully hoped that students on campuses around the country would concentrate their energies on organizations such as the Intercollegiate Liberal Club and the League for Industrial Democracy. "These serious movements," he argued, "... are of a significance which already affords a respectable counterpoise to the tendencies which manifest themselves so unfruitfully in the spectacular defiance of reverence, decorum, and restraint." College students paid little attention to such statements and joined other youth in the frolic of fun. The college campuses of the period became the center for the Rah-Rah boys who joined fraternities, attended football games, and saw college as a place to have a good time. Of course, this was not different from many other periods in college history, but during the 1920s, the numbers involved increased significantly with greater college attendance. The college style would come into full domination later in the

1960s when over 40 percent of the youth population would be in school.

The frivolous style of life associated with youth in the 1920s came to an abrupt end with the beginning of the Depression of the 1930s. The Depression impressed Americans with the fact that youth had become marginal in terms of economic production. Unemployed youth became one of the central issues of the Depression. Like other marginal groups, such as blacks, youth found itself the last hired and the first fired. Lacking the seasoned skills of older workers, it became more and more difficult during a time of high unemployment for youth to obtain jobs. The 1940 census revealed that by the end of the Depression, 35 percent of the unemployed were youth under the age of twenty-five, whereas only 22 percent of the employable population was within that age range.

In response to the crises of the Depression the American Council on Education established an American Youth Commission to investigate the problems of young America and offer any possible solutions. In 1937 the Chairman of the American Youth Council offered the following portrait of the condition of the young in America. Defining youth as between sixteen and twenty-four, he described a mythical town of Youngville with a population of 200 youths. Within this town 76 youths had regular jobs, 40 went to school or college, 5 went to school part time, 28 were married women, and 51 were out of work and out of school. Half of those out of work received federal aid. The Chairman claimed that Youngville was also experiencing a major decline in health rate. According to the statistics of the Youth Commission, one out of four among young America had syphilis or gonorrhea and 5 percent were presently, would be, or had been in an asylum. Added to these problems was the highest crime rate in the country.

The chairman dramatized the conditions of the young by comparing them to those existing in Italy and Germany before the rise of fascism. Echoing the general concern during the Depression about rising fascism in America, he argued, "It will need education and organization and vigorous action among the young people and those devoted to their care and education to save America from fascism, and youth from becoming storm troops for an American dictator." Democracy, he claimed, must provide equal opportunity for all of its citizens. How this equal opportunity was to be extended within the framework of the existing economic and technological structure was not made clear. The only hope, without a major change in industrial progress, was for the government to create jobs for the young outside the existing industrial structure. Like schools and clubs, this became another form of institutionalization.

It was in the context of filling the gap caused by technological advances and the economic conditions of the Depression that the federal government swung into action to solve the problem of youth. Howard Bell stated, in a survey of the conditions of young people conducted under the auspices of the American Youth Commission in the 1930s, that the major problem for youth was what will 21 million young Americans "do with themselves during the ever-widening period between the time when the schools are through with them and jobs are ready for them?" The federal government responded in 1933 by establishing the Civilian Conservation Corps (CCC), which gave fulltime work to young men between the ages of eighteen and twenty-five and housing near their work projects. In 1935 the National Youth Administration (NYA) was established to provide part-time employment for both men and women who lived at home and maintained their normal community lives. During the Depression both programs combined to give some employment to over 5 million youth. The CCC reported in 1940 that during the 1930s it had given employment to 2½ million young men, 84 percent of whom were under nineteen years of age. The NYA arranged employment for out-of-school youth and developed student work programs for in-school students.

The efforts of the CCC and the NYA were justified in terms of what was called the new or Keynesian economics. During periods of slow economic growth it was argued the federal government should stimulate the economy by increased spending on public projects. During the Depression much of this federal spending was directed toward civilian needs. After World War II, defense spending became the major economic stimulator. The work of the CCC and NYA involved the construction of thousands of public projects, such as rural schools, workshops, community centers, post offices, parks, airports, and recreation centers. Women were employed in clerical and service activities in schools, hospitals, libraries, and social agencies.

The Depression reinforced and strengthened the identity of youth as a special group within society. Before and after World War I the schools, popular literature, and advertising had begun to separate youth from other age groups in terms of tastes, modes of expression, and dress. Certainly the flapper period of the 1920s can be seen as an expression of a growing youth culture. What happened during the Depression was that this identity centered around economic interests. Youth perceived they were a special economic class with specific economic problems. When Howard Bell surveyed the youth of Maryland in the 1930s as a representative sample of all American youth, he found "that only one-fourth of the youth believed that there was *no* youth problem. . . ." Bell reported that 57.7 percent of the youth surveyed claimed economic security as the major problem for young people in America. Some of the comments recorded by Bell suggested how younger members of the population were gaining a sense of identity. One youth in the survey stated, "The youth of America will have to wake up and organize themselves. Other people won't help if youth does nothing for itself. . . ." Another complained, "Youth is in a muddle. Out of school too young; they don't know what they want to do or why. They are in the midst of a great social and economic change."

World War II provided a temporary solution to both the youth problem and the Depression. War industries and the armed forces absorbed the economic problems and the young. For the first time in the twentieth century school enrollments for those between the ages of five and twenty-one began to decline. Enrollments for those between five and seventeen peaked in 1940 at 94.1 percent and steadily declined during the war until 1944, when 89 percent of that age group was in school. College attendance for those between eighteen and twenty-one declined from 15.6 percent in 1940 to 11.9 percent in 1946. The decline in enrollments was a direct consequence of the fact that during times of war, youth suddenly had a useful function to fullfill both in terms of fighting battles and working industry. For those between the ages of fourteen and nineteen, involvement in the labor force increased from 44 percent in 1940 to 69.2 percent in 1944.

The only important lesson that appeared to have been learned during World War II was that service in the armed forces was one way of keeping youth occupied. Influenced by both real and imaginary threats, the United States instituted a peacetime draft that included a series of deferments that allowed for exemption from military service if one went to college or obtained a job in the national interest. Another important consequence of the war was the establishment of a GI Bill that provided returning veterans with the opportunity of returning to college. The effect of the draft, the GI Bill, and the fact that neither the Depression nor the war had integrated youth into the social and economic structure of America was the extension of the custodial role of the school into the college years. College enrollments for those between eighteen and twenty-one increased to 17.6 percent in 1946 and jumped again in 1956 to 31.2 percent. By 1965 college enrollments for the eighteen to twenty-one-year-old group was absorbing 43.9 percent of that population.

Immediately following the war educators were anxious that youth who had been able to find employment in war industries return to school. Launching a back-to-school campaign in the early years following the war, many educators were disheartened that youth could still find jobs. The General Secretary of the National Child Labor Committee complained in the early part of 1947, "With jobs still to be had, the young people who left school for work during the war have not returned to school to any noticeable degree and their ranks continue to be augmented by new school-leavers." Interestingly, the secretary suggested, "Short of a depression—and unemployment is a costly price to pay for increased school attendance—most of these young workers are lost to the schools for good." During the spring of 1949 unemployment of both adults and young people increased seriously. The marginality of youth was again shown; while the general unemployment rate was 5 percent, it was around 14 percent for youth between sixteen and nineteen years of age. The changes in the employment market were again reflected in school enrollment figures. In 1946 the percentage of those between the ages of five and seventeen who were enrolled in school was 90.3. In 1948 the percentage dropped to 89.5, and by 1950 it increased to 92.6. After 1950 this percentage steadily increased, except for a slight drop between 1958 and 1960, until it reached 97.1 percent in 1965.

The postwar youth population had grown up during the Depression, had survived the ordeals of the war years, and were to see peace only in terms of cold war. Those who had comprised the youth population of the 1930s approached middle age following the war, and they viewed things from a different perspective from the new younger generation. During the Depression the most important concern was economic security, and during the postwar period, the new older generation hoped to realize this goal. But for the new younger generation the postwar years were ones of disillusionment and a feeling of being beat. Around 1950 Jack Kerouc voiced the feelings of the younger generation with, "You know, this really is a beat generation." The generation was beat from the Depression, the war, and the feeling the peace that was inherited was only as secure as the next headline. Author Cellon Holmes wrote in an article "This Is the Beat Generation," which appeared in the *New York Times Magazine* in 1952, that beat meant "More than mere weariness, it implies the feeling of having been used, of being raw. It involves a sort of nakedness of mind, and, ulti-mately, of soul; a feeling of being reduced to the bedrock of consciousness. In short, it means being undramatically pushed up against the wall." The new generation, Holmes argued, lived in a world of shattered ideals and accepted the mud in the moral currents. "They were brought up in these ruins," he wrote, "and no longer notice them. They drink to 'come down' or to 'get high' not to illustrate anything. Their excursions into drugs or promiscuity come out of curiosity, not disillusion-ment." But he felt that beneath the detachment, there was a desperate quest for belief. The quest for belief was to become a major factor in the generation of the 1960s.

Beat culture was only one aspect of the youth culture after World War II. The other was life in the inner cities following the war. New urban conditions were again responded to by edu-cators in terms of keeping youth in school. The urban problems following the war were in the context of an entirely different set of population changes. By the 1950s Americans had learned to accept a predominantly urban culture, but a new concern was raised that cities in America were dying. The mass exodus to the suburbs following World War II caused a decrease in population in most of the central areas of major cities. Between 1950 and 1960 the central area of New York decreased in pop-ulation by 1.4 percent, while the population around the central city increased by 75 percent. The demographic changes in New York were typical of other large cities. Chicago experienced a decline of 1.9 percent in the central city and a 71.5 percent in-crease outside the central area; Boston's central city occupants were reduced by 13 percent, Cleveland lost 4.2 percent, Detroit 9.7 percent, and St. Louis 12.5 percent. In all of these cases the population jumped more than 50 percent in areas surrounding the central city. The exodus to suburban areas was mainly by white middle-class and upper-middle-class groups that left the poor and what educators called "culturally deprived" to occupy the central city. A study of the 1960 census revealed a signifi-cant difference between the average educational level of those living in the central city and those living on the urban fringe. The average for all urbanized areas for those with 4 years of high school or more living in the central city was 40.9 percent, for central city nonwhites it was 28.3 percent, and for residents on the urban fringe it was 50.9 percent.

Educators defined the aiding of a frustrated underprivileged youth in the central cities as one of their primary tasks. Black students in the cities were particularly frustrated by the feeling that they had to attend a school that taught subjects that to them were not relevant and were dominated by the traditions of a surrounding white society. Added to this frustration was the realization that most occupations would be closed to him when he left school. James Bryant Conant reported in *Slums and Suburbs* in 1961 that in one of America's largest cities, 59 percent of the male youth between the ages of sixteen and twenty-one were out of school and unemployed. In another city slum area a sampling of the youth population revealed 70 percent of the boys and girls ages sixteen to twenty-one were out of school and unemployed. Conant wrote, "In such a situation, the pupil may ask, 'Why bother to stay in school when graduation for half the boys opens onto a dead-end street?'"

Like the educators at the beginning of the century, those in the 1960s stated as one of their goals the retention of youth in the schools. Conant reiterated an old theme when he wrote, "A youth who has dropped out of school and never has had a full-time job is not likely to become a constructive citizen of his community. . . . As a frustrated individual he is likely to be anti-social and is rebellious, and may well become a juvenile delinquent." Black urban youth not only lacked a functional social role, but also saw little prospect of future employment or meaningful social status. Educators believed that for education to be meaningful to the urban poor, some prospect of success and of the application of education had to be provided. To prevent what he called the "social dynamite" of the cities from going off, Conant recommended that jobs be provided and that education be geared to preparing for them. Efforts had to be made to expand economic opportunities for the entire black community. Conant maintained, "It was no good whatever to prepare boys and girls for nonexistent jobs."

Some educators during the 1960s still maintained a certain antagonism toward city life. Conant compared the country to the city and looked with horror on the street life of the city child. In a revealing statement, Conant emphasized that the "boys brought up in slum neighborhoods, even if they come to the big city from the country as children, are conditioned to street life with all that this life implies." But this antagonism was balanced by a growing recognition that the street life of children and the advantages of urban culture could be utilized in the organization of educational programs. In the first place it was argued that rural white Protestant ideas could not be used to teach poor urban children. The material and activities of the urban school had to be based on the values and life of the child outside of the school. Harold Howe, the United States Commissioner of Education, echoed this growing awareness among educators in 1967 when he argued that traditionally American schools worked from the basis of white, middle-class, Anglo-Saxon ideas that worked reasonably well when the lessons of the school were reinforced by the lessons of the home. But these ideas, he claimed, ". . . are so alien to the lives of the millions of disadvantaged urban children who fill our city schools today, there is a vast psychological distance between the clientele of today's urban schools . . . and the suppliers of education-teachers, administrators, and school board members." Secondly, educators began to realize most urban children did not have the opportunity to explore fully their own urban world. Instead of taking the children to the country, educators began to talk about taking the children across town to the city aquarium or art institute.

The conditions of the inner cities were just one aspect of the continuing problem of youth. The expansion of industrial development with automated systems caused an even further decrease in the social usefulness of youth. Conant noted in 1961 that the unemployment rate for youth under twenty-one was twice the nationwide rate for all workers. This figure did not include those enrolled in college, whose numbers increased rapidly following World War II. The increase in college attendance was the result of increased requirements for jobs and the fact the economy could support a larger number of people not participating in production. What had begun with the rise of the urban industrial complex at the beginning of the century reached new heights. At the turn of the century the expansion of the custodial role of the school had increased the length of economic dependency of children on their families. After World War II, the length of dependency extended through the college years for middle-class and upper-middle-class youth. The city had reduced the social usefulness of children, and modern industry reduced their productive usefulness. During the course of the twentieth century, this phenomenon extended beyond the city. Even on farms, as machinery replaced much of the work, children became less useful and more dependent.

Youth in the modern world became a social group that existed in a state of dependency, not like slaves to produce but to consume. Youth was not needed to participate in the production of goods, but it was needed for their consumption. Secondary schools and colleges delayed and prepared youth for future entrance into production, occupied their time, kept them out of trouble, and made them available for consumption. Locked in institutions, they were exploited by a host of consumer fads. Automobile companies, music corporations, clothing industries, and numbers of other manufacturers designed products for this new social group.

The combination of extended dependency, consumer exploitation, and the sharing of a common social life helped to create a youth culture. But it was not a culture that remained content with being socially important only in terms of consumption and future production. As a social group free of concern about working, it could define its social importance in terms of humanitarian crusades. Beginning in the early 1960s, youth joined with blacks to launch a massive civil rights campaign. During the middle 1960s youth began to define their social role by participation in civil rights campaigns, battles against pollution, political campaigns, and a variety of other social projects. Youth, by the end of the 1960s, freed from concerns about work, was attempting to become socially useful by directing its energy to the problems of society.

The schools were not prepared for the emergence of this new social role. Acting as custodial institutions they were organized around the assumption that youth had no important social role. Much of the turmoil in the high schools and colleges in the industrial countries of the world during the 1960s was the result of a conflict between youth's newly defined social function and the older social role of the school. If youth was to be kept in school and maintain its new social role, the school had to change. The accommodation on the part of the school had to take the form of allowing for direct social involvement. In high schools and colleges students demanded that their institutions become actively committed to participation in social change. The organizations that had helped to create the social status of youth were called on to reorganize and to provide an institutional outlet for student activism. One sign of how some schools, mostly universities, began to adapt was the allowing of students in the fall of 1970 to use class time for participation in political campaigns. Senator Charles Percy argued before the 1970 United States Senate that the national interest that once demanded a summer vacation from school so that the young could work in the harvest now demanded a fall break so that the young could help harvest the votes. By the mid-1970's, however, concern again was expressed about the redundancy and the conformity of youth.

chapter five

the search for alternatives

Americans in the 1960s witnessed a serious challenge to the continued growth of the public school in the United States. At a time when President Lyndon B. Johnson was using the schools to wage a war on poverty, others were demanding that traditional public schools be abolished. Criticism of the schools had existed from their beginnings, but it was always in terms of either the curriculum, method of instruction, or organization of the school. Educators always sought reform within the context of the school and did not seriously question the very existence of the school. Ivan Illich, in a lecture at the Yale Divinity School in 1970, compared the educational reformer to the frustrated driver in a traffic jam who dreams of solving the problem by adding new lanes to the highway. Illich believed, "It is not the present school system which is obsolete, but the very idea of one institution which provides society with education." It was recognized by Illich that attacking the school at such a basic level was heresy to those who viewed the school as others had viewed the church. Several centuries of growth in the United States had convinced people that the school was a necessary and permanent feature of American society. Any basic attack on the school was comparable to religious heresy.

There were a host of attempts to develop alternative forms of educational systems during the 1960s. What were called free schools took root throughout the country and quickly began to develop their own forms of national organization. By 1970 there was already developing an embryonic bureaucratic structure in the form of an information center about free schools in Santa Barbara, California and a Canadian-based magazine devoted to articles about the free school movement. Numbers of Americans went to Cuernavaca, Mexico to attend the lectures on alternative forms of education given at the Center for Intercultural Documentation. A radical education project that distributed information and articles on the new education throughout the country was centered in Ann Arbor, Michigan. In 1969 the Canadian journal *This Magazine is about Schools* was able to publish a list of over 70 free schools in the United States and Canada. Many of the free schools came into being without any particular plan and with only a common feeling that something had to be done. For instance, the founders of the Shaker Mountain School in Vermont reported in 1969 that, "We started a school in Vermont last year. We had $30 and a car. It was a Plymouth, so we thought about calling it "The Plymouth School" but we finally named it after the mountain behind our farm—Shaker Mountain School." If there was any model for the free school, it was A. S. Neill's Summerhill school, begun in England earlier in the century.

While it was not all together clear at all times what the free schools were doing, there was a general consensus about what was wrong with public school education. In general the movement was sparked by a reaction against the custodial nature of the schools that appeared to be preparing the students for manipulation by a war-oriented and exploitive society. There was a general concern that the institutional nature of the schools bred a conformist personality that too easily fitted into the corporate structure of American society. It appeared that the educational system placed more of an emphasis on preparing the individual to meet social needs than individual development. For the critics the school had become merely a method for social grading and a preparation for an authoritarian society.

Three of the leading critics of education were Paul Goodman, Edgar Z. Friedenberg, and Ivan Illich. During the early 1960s Goodman delivered a series of lectures and speeches questioning America's basic faith in increased schooling. Goodman recounted in the preface to his book *Compulsory Mis-Education* that at one educational meeting when he suggested there was already too much formal schooling "and that, under present conditions, the more we get the less education we will get," the others looked at him oddly and proceeded to discuss how to get more money for schools. Goodman claimed he realized "suddenly that I am confronting a mass superstition." His criticism of the functioning of the school centered around what he perceived to be its noneducational role in society. What he attacked were the very concerns that had led to the increased expansion of the role of the school in the early part of the twentieth century. Goodman expressed concern that the school had attempted to take over the activities of the family with its apparent collapse in urban centers, solve the problem of the nonfunctional role of youth in modern society, and meet the needs of a highly specialized modern industrial world. In Goodman's words, these concerns had turned the schools into "a baby-sitting service during a period of collapse of the old-type family" and "an arm of the police, providing cops and concentration camps paid for in the budget under the heading 'Board of Education.' " The major educational role had become, according to Goodman, "to provide—at public and parents' expense—apprentice-training for corporations, government, and the teaching profession itself...."

Goodman believed that the increased social functions of the school had detracted from what he defined as its true aim of getting "one out of his isolated class and into the one humanity." When in 1964 the Secretary of Labor proposed extending compulsory education to the age of eighteen, Goodman called the proposal "a device to keep the unemployed off the streets by putting them into concentration camps called schools." He claimed it was fallacious to maintain the argument that there was a direct connection between employability and years of education. That this connection existed was a result, he argued, of a self-proving myth held by educators and employers. Goodman maintained that it was closer to the truth to see the link as being between social class and the type of job youth was able to obtain. From his standpoint lower-class children got lower-class jobs, middle-class children tended to get middle-class jobs, and upper-class children by and large got the type of jobs held within their social class. The link between education and job types was the result of the number of years of education. According to Goodman, extended schooling with its selective process benefited a few great corporations that chose those who scored highest in the school race.

Goodman wanted education to shed its custodial and corporate training functions and direct its energies toward helping people to live in a highly technological society with a greater concern for the quality of technological expansion and for the quality and value of social organizations. In terms of educational history Goodman placed himself in the same tradition as John Dewey. Goodman maintained that Dewey's brand of progressive education "was the first thoroughgoing analysis of the crucial modern problem . . . of how to cope with high industrialism and scientific technology which are strange to people. . . ." If, he stated, "progressive education had been generally adopted, we should not be so estranged and ignorant today." The problem was that progressive theory had been perverted when it was applied in public and private schools. The schools used Dewey's progressivism to expand the curriculum into areas that avoided the crucial problems. "The practical training and community democracy," Goodman wrote, "whose purpose was to live scientifically and change society, was changed into 'socially useful' subjects and a psychology of 'belonging.'"

Goodman's major shortcoming was that he did not offer any

significant alternatives in educational philosophy. He was trapped by the same arguments used by liberal educators throughout the twentieth century. Goodman did claim one major departure from Dewey's progressivism, and that was the demand for greater freedom. As trustee of a Summerhill variant school in the United States, he was influenced by A. S. Neill's argument that a child should have the freedom to attend or not attend a class. Neill asserted, Goodman wrote, "a principle that to Dewey did not seem important, the freedom to choose to go to class or stay away altogether." Goodman argued that this was the major departure in progressive education that was catching on in America and creating the fight against compulsory education. He attacked compulsory education as being "no longer designed for the maximum growth and future practical utility of the children into a changing world, but . . . rather inept social engineering for extrinsic goals, pitifully short-range." What Goodman failed to realize was that social engineering and social control were as much a part of Dewey as communitarian democracy.

In *Compulsory Mis-Education* Goodman proposed some important changes in the organization of schools. Some of these proposals were designed to decentralize and deprofessionalize the educational system. For urban areas he suggested that large schools be replaced by tiny schools of the storefront variety equipped with record player and pinball machines to allow for formal and informal activities. In some cases, he felt the children should be taught outside of the school using streets, movies, museums, factories, and unlicensed adults of the community, such as the druggist, the storekeeper, and the mechanic. These were not radical proposals; they were within the progressive tradition of making the school a community and using the resources of the larger community as resources in education. Goodman's major departure was again in terms of compulsory education. He proposed that class attendance be made voluntary and that a form of GI Bill be designed that would give school money directly to the high school age adolescents "for any plausible self-chosen educational proposals, such as purposeful travel or individual enterprise."

While Goodman was directing his attack against compulsory education, Edgar Z. Friedenberg was analyzing the effect of institutional life in the schools on the development of adolescents. His two most significant works were *The Vanishing Adolescent*, published in 1959, and *Coming of Age in America*, published in 1965. Of the two major works *Coming of Age in America* was the most important in terms of the institutional effect of the school. This work contained a description and analysis of a very imaginative set of tests designed to indicate the type of values that were being fostered within the school. One test began with a problem situation where a teacher found a student who was known as a troublemaker smoking in the school lavatory. The high school students taking the test were asked to select several best responses by the teacher and several worst responses. The choices ranged from the teacher hitting the student to the teacher doing nothing. The most popular response given by high school students tested by Friedenberg was for the teacher to discuss the problem with the school psychologist who agreed "to get at Johnny's 'antisocial' behavior and straighten him out."

One of the important things Friedenberg pointed out about the results of this test was that high school students themselves tended to define "normal" behavior as that behavior condoned by the institution. Deviation from the standards of the school was defined as abnormal behavior requiring psychological treatment. Friedenberg also discovered, using this test and others, that schooling created the image of American society as being ruled by benign institutions. All actions by the school administration, by school psychologists, and by teachers were defined by the students as attempts to help the individual. This occurred even when it appeared that the school was acting in a destructive fashion. Because of this view of the benignancy of institutions, most students believed it was the duty of parents and pupils to cooperate with school officials at all times. Friedenberg compared this attitude with the workings of American foreign policy, where foreign aid was given with the attitude that the officials of the country receiving the aid should now cooperate by accepting the activities of the American military and intelligence personnel. "We are disposed," Friedenberg wrote, "to regard as hostile those neutralist governments that tell us firmly to keep out and permit them to manage their own affairs; we assume that they have some inherent obligation to cooperate with the 'Free World.' "

What students learned within the school, Friedenberg argued, was that to advance in society one must conform one's behavior to the rules of institutions and accept as a model of good character the ability to follow institutional procedures. This meant institutional structures in American society were the new standards for social judgment and, at best, they placed efficiency of procedure over other values. Students within the school were also taught that they were without rights and only had privileges. The student entered school and was given privileges that could arbitrarily be revoked by school officials. Students never felt they had certain basic rights the school could not infringe on. Friedenberg argued that compulsory education laws were a classic example of this condition. He described compulsory education as the requirement that a student be "in a specific place, under the charge of a particular group of persons in whose selection they have no voice, performing tasks about which they have no choice, without remuneration and subject to specialized regulations and sanctions that are applicable to no one else in the community." Because of compulsory education, Friedenberg argued, one of the first things the young learn in school is "that they do not participate fully in the freedoms guaranteed by the state, and that therefore, these freedoms do not really partake of the character of inalienable rights."

Friedenberg was not only concerned about institutional conformity and what the young learned about civil rights in American society, but also about the specific type of values supported and given recognition by the school. These values, he believed, reflected a lower-middle-class conformist style of life that excluded the poor, the rich, and the creative. These latter groups received no support for their life-styles within the framework of the school. It was in the context of this concern about the identity problem of adolescents that Friedenberg offered several alternative forms of education.

Friedenberg shared Goodman's belief that one of the first things that had to be accomplished was the abolition of compulsory education. He suggested youth be treated in the same fashion as farmers by the government. "Farmers are provided," he wrote, "with a wealth of technical services of high quality that they are free to ignore, and subsidized against the economic catastrophe that would otherwise result from their ignoring it." Following Goodman's line of thinking he proposed that a form of GI bill be established. For the poor, he suggested, the alternative should be offered of a residential instituition that would not attempt to indoctrinate the students into middle-class behavior, but would provide a warmer and richer environment for living. He reasoned that the academic problems of the poor were primarily the result of a wretched home environment. Noncompulsory public schools would continue to exist with the option open that the student could use the money designated for a public school at a private institution or boarding school.

Goodman's and Friedenberg's concern with breaking the monopolistic control of education by the public schools was shared by the Mexican-based educational reformer, Ivan Illich. The main thrust of Illich's criticism extended beyond public schools alone to the whole concept of schooling itself. During the late 1950s Illich was vice-chancellor of the Catholic University of Puerto Rico and a member of the Commonwealth Board of Higher Education. Both the experience Illich had in Puerto Rico and his work, beginning in 1961, of training missionaires and volunteers for service in Latin America convinced him that the importation of established forms of educational systems into underdeveloped countries would have a negative effect upon the social progress of those areas. As one of the cofounders of the Center for Intercultural Documentation in Cuernavaca, Mexico, Illich organized during the springs of 1970 and 1971 a series of lectures given by leading educational critics throughout the world on alternative forms of education.

Schooling, as defined by Illich, was an institutional structure that exercised obligatory custodial control for the purpose of teaching within the framework of a graded curriculum. Illich argued that the effect of the graded curriculum was to create the illusion that educational progress was the result of moving from one grade level to another. Of equal importance was the creation of the myth that all education was the result of schooling. Schooling had the important social function of instilling into the population the basic social beliefs of society and providing for ritual certification. The important thing about the certification process, Illich believed, was that if people believed in schooling, they accepted the level of certification given them by the school. Schooling not only created the myth that all education was schooling, but also that the only fair means of determining social position was through schooling.

Illich argued that the key to the Age of Schooling was faith, the same type of faith that supported the medieval church as a place for all men. The church promised equality in heaven while supporting a highly stratified and economically exploitive life here on earth. The school promised educational equality while economically exploiting the lower classes and assuring the continued existence of social inequalities. Nowhere was this more clearly shown, Illich maintained, than in Latin America. He claimed, in an article in the *Saturday Review* in 1968, that no government in South America spent less than 18 percent of its budget on schools and that some spent more than 30 percent. But with this large percentage of state monies, only a small percentage of the population was fully aided. Nowhere in Latin America did more than 27 percent get beyond the sixth grade or more than 1 percent graduate from universities. Those who graduated from the universities were generally from upper-middle-class and upper-class families who could have afforded the education without state support. This was a point Illich stressed in a commencement address given at the University of Puerto Rico in the late 1960s. Illich told the graduates, "The graduation rite that we solemnly celebrate today confirms the prerogatives which Puerto Rican society, by means of a costly system of subsidized public schools, confers upon the sons and daughters of its most privileged citizens." He emphasized that they represented the privileged 10 percent of their generation in Puerto Rico who were able to complete their university studies. "Public investment," Illich told them, "in each of you is fifteen times the educational investment in the average member of the poorest ten percent of the population, who drops out of school before completing the fifth grade."

Once the mythology of schooling is accepted, Illich maintained, the poor believe they are poor because they did not make it through school. The acceptance of this position was more strongly felt because they believed and were told they were given the opportunity for advancement. Social position was translated by schooling into achievement and under-achievement. Within the school the social and economic advantages of the rich became educational achievement. The social and economic disadvantages of the poor became under-achievement. The school created dropouts. Dropouts did not exist without the school. The school therefore acted as a powerful instrument of social condemnation and acceptance, because everyone believed in the school. In a well-schooled society, Illich argued, people are schooled into their social places. If they felt frustrated by their status, they were referred to other forms of schooling, such as night or trade school. If the individual did not take this advantage, then his continued exclusion from a higher social status became his own fault. If he did, he found he made minor economic gains and learned that he could not go much further because he did not take advantage of school while young. In either case he was forced to accept what he was as his own failure.

Illich's concern with schooling extended beyond the problems of the poor. Western culture itself was trapped by the whole mythology of education being a function of schooling. From Illich's point of view the United States, along with other countries, had to go through a period of deschooling. He recognized that deschooling society would not be easy. Illich suggested in the speech at the Yale Divinity School that eliminating school teachers would be as difficult as eliminating the practitioners of the world's oldest profession. Some people would always find it easier to buy and sell love and learning instead of to develop the real thing. In strong words, Illich told his audience at Yale, "...once the red bricks of the schoolhouse are seen in the red light of the whorehouse, laws will be passed to protect or at least tolerate the personal weaknesses of adult citizens, so long as the young and the weak are not forced to visit either professional teachers or professional prostitutes."

Goodman, Friedenberg, and Illich were all popular reading with those involved in the free school movement. While the three men provided literature on what to avoid, there was little direction given to the general movement. The hope still seemed to exist that some form of education would bring about radical social change. The free schools that followed the Summerhill model hoped that the good society would result when all would be given the freedom to develop naturally. These schools worked within a tradition dating back to at least Rousseau that education should be freedom to develop natural virtues and talents. Others hoped to use education as a means for developing the right social values within each individual. For instance, in the 1960s one of the problems the founders of a day nursery at the University of Toronto felt they had to overcome was the possessiveness and greed of children. Within their minds was the hope of achieving a more radical form of communitarian society than had been sought by Dewey. However, even their attempts represented no major departure from educational experiments of the past.

Placed in the framework of educational history of the twentieth century, the reform work of the 1960s can be seen as offering a more direct challenge and criticism of public schools than other movements of the past, but not necessarily any unique alternatives. In fact, many of the school experiments of the 1960s had direct predecessors in educational experiments conducted in the 1920s. This earlier period was rich in attempts to develop alternative forms of education of which Summerhill was but one product. Many of these experiments might have lasted if the economic upheaval caused by the Depression had not forced most of them to close. Many of the growth pains of the free school movement in the 1960s might have been avoided if its members had paid greater attention to the efforts of the past.

The Walden and Manumit schools of the 1920s are only two of a vast number of schools that are part of the free school tradition. They represent two different models that could have been used for edification by the free school movement of the 1960s. The Walden School was an attempt to develop an education that provided maximum freedom for the child. The Manumit School represented an effort to design an educational plan for the children of workers. Both of these schools ran counter to the society-centered progressivism that had found expression in the *Cardinal Principles* and that was shaping the public schools in the 1920s.

Margaret Naumburg, the founder of Walden School in New York City, was concerned about the materialistic and conformist values that seemed to be pervading American society in the 1920s. One of the problems highlighted by Naumburg's educational interests was the relationship between individual action and the needs of group life. This was one of the basic problems in any effort to use education as a tool of social reform. In the United States in the 1920s the debate ranged across all possibilities. On one end of the spectrum was the argument that the traditional American emphasis on economic individualism created a competitive society that destroyed a feeling of community as well as a sense of individual responsibility for the welfare of fellow men. It was often pointed out that competition within the school for grades, honors, and athletic achievement conditioned the pupil to act only for his self-advancement without regard for other men. On the other end of the spectrum it was argued that the group life of the school destroyed individualism and created the conformity of a mass society. The schools were taken to task for imposing standardized codes of conduct, promoting group activity, and subordinating individual personality for the good of the institution. Of course, no one concerned about this problem adopted any hard and fast position at one end of the spectrum, because all saw the necessity of achieving some sort of balance between the two positions. It would also be overly simplistic to consider the debate as merely one between individualism and conformity. All thought they were promoting individualism.

Margaret Naumburg differed radically from other educational innovators who were working within the public schools at that time. She did agree with them that traditional forms of rote learning, sit-at-your-desk tasks, grades, and other mechanical school activities had to be replaced. Where she differed from them was in the type of social world they were trying to achieve through their educational changes. In general Naumburg was concerned about the brand of society-centered progressive education found in public schools, which sought to reform social and economic conditions by creating a highly organized economic and social structure where individualism found expression through contributions to group activity. Within the matrix of this view of society, the school had the function of socializing the individual so that he would define his own interests in terms of the interests of the group. Some of the major concerns were centered around abolishing the competitive aspects of schooling, introducing clubs and group activities in the schoolroom, promoting extracurricular activities, and in general teaching the student to work within one organization so that he would function well in larger organizations. It was a common feeling among public schoolmen that a student's social record or citizenship grade was more important than his academic grade, because the grade represented only individual achievement while the other represented a more important accomplishment of being able to function well in a group.

Margaret Naumburg believed this trend in education was developing a herd instinct in man and was completely submerging the individual in the life of the group. To her this form of education was only perpetuating the materialistic and businessman mentality of American life. Like many other Americans of the time she reacted against the self-seeking, hypocritical businessman's world of the 1920s. In the *New Republic* in 1930 she stated that it was difficult to develop a philosophy of individualism in America "because America is so group-minded, any questioning as to the positive value of this constant and limited herd life is sure to be a source of irritation." Naumburg believed that America's "instinctive faith in the power of groups to change the face of the world is still so unchallenged that we are incapable, as a nation of realizing the strength that may yet lie in a more individualized life."

Writing in 1928 Naumburg stated her belief that in the schools the first concern was not with human beings, but with producing a particular type of society. To a great extent she held John Dewey responsible for both the group activity emphasis of education and the social emphasis of the schools. While recognizing the great contributions of Dewey in reforming the curriculum, nevertheless she felt he had done great harm in not developing an adequate philosophy of individualism. Dewey's problem in Naumburg's words was that, "to him the individualism of the past is inevitably tied to the laissez-faire economics of Big Business; and this he dismisses briefly as unproductive to the group of our future social order." Naumburg argued that Dewey's brand of individualism erroneously was considered as a product of social relationships and publicly acknowledged functions. Naumburg described the world Dewey wanted as, "A dull and gloomy picture, this technological utopia, to those of us who still hope for a richer and socially balanced individualism—the flowering of a more equitable society."

Naumburg believed that the schools had failed to recognize the rich emotional and inner life of each individual. Influenced by psychoanalytical theory, and particularly by Jungian psychology, she claimed each individual had a subjective inner life that coexisted and was coessential with the life of social action. Each child, she maintained, was born with a life force that intertwined itself with the life of the world. "Existence," she wrote, "always consists of a double rhythm, a swing of energy out towards the world and a pull back from the world to the 'ego' again." Speaking through the person of a director of a modern school in a 1928 article in *Survey* she stated her objection to Dewey and the behaviorists for their reduction of all emotional and psychic states to environmental or social conditions. Naumburg did not reject the importance of group activity, but saw each group of individuals as having a unique inner life of its own through which the inner life of the individual gained expression.

The Walden School emphasized creative and artistic expression as a means of developing the inner life of the child. The school was noted for its work in painting, dramatics, and creative writing. The work in Walden School was viewed as a way of drawing out and expressing the uniqueness of each individual. Naumburg's Walden School, by placing its emphasis on this aspect of development, represented a break with the major thrust of educational change in the public schools. She rejected the notion that uniqueness and individuality were a function of one's social role and contribution to society. This was also a rejection of the corporate world, which sought efficiency by having a smoothly functioning industrial machine where the schools supplied men with needed skills and a social training that prepared them to merge their personality with that of the industrial state. Naumburg represented a major dissenter from the traditionally heavy American emphasis on the social purposes of education.

The very existence of a school for worker's children challenged the traditional goals of the common school. Manumit attempted to provide an education for a particular social class. During the 1920s the New York State Federation of Labor established a model school for worker's children at Pawling, New York, and organized Pioneer Youth Clubs for boys and girls from the ages of seven to eighteen. The educational planks of New York State Federation of Labor's platform stated two major goals for the future development of education. One goal reflected the awesome experience of the destruction of World War I and the continued international armaments race following the War. The platform called for the rewriting of textbooks to eliminate "the glorification of war and to substitute the facts about war; its cold-blooded butchery ... its misery because of economic chaos and its debts which bear so heavily upon the workers for the benefit of the profiteers and munition makers and financiers." The New York platform also directed its attention to what it referred to as the "deadening" effect of the regimented public schools. The schools of the future, it stated "must be built on freedom and cooperation, must liberate and organize the capacities of children. . . ."

The model school for worker's children was called Manumit and was established in 1924 on a 177-acre farm with a well-stocked herd of cattle, a trout stream, and a school garden. The general purpose of the school was to arouse public opinion, as one staff member stated, so that "labor can exercise an influence of incalculable importance in modifying and reviving the public school system." The children who attended were from nine to seventeen years old, and all had parents who

were union members. The school was planned as a self-govern-
ing community with each student having equal voice in the
management of school affairs. When Manumit opened in 1924,
a writer in the *Nation* reported that the words "A New Social
Order" ran through all discussions about the outcome of the
school's activities and was, in the writers words, "a bright
cord of faith on which all other things of life are strung."

The general organization of the school was designed to avoid
the militaristic regimentation of the public schools, to free the
child by avoiding authoritarian teaching, and to eliminate social competition by reducing academic competition. Statements by the school stressed that the students would not be
indoctrinated into any particular ideology, but would be allowed the freedom to develop their own ideas and ideals. In
many ways the spirit of the school centered around Dewey's
ideal of a communitarian democracy. The school was to be a
community where one learned the necessity for social cooperation and an interdependent society. One of the early statements from the school stressed, "The community school is our
way of affirming our deep belief in Dewey's maxim that education comes through life." Being a residential school it could
more fully exploit the community ideal than the public school
could. A staff member reported in 1927 one incident in the life
of the school that exemplified the type of social education the
students were learning. One morning when the residents arrived for breakfast, they found it was not to be served because
a member of the supper squad the previous evening had gone
on strike and refused to clean the dishes. A general meeting
was immediately called and it was learned that the dishes had
been cleaned, but not by the group assigned to the task. This
action violated the constitution of the community. The community divided between the constitutionalists who demanded
no breakfast and those who wanted to introduce a motion
allowing breakfast to be served. Breakfast was eventually
served and the lesson of cooperative democratic action was
learned, according to the staff member.

The fact that Manumit did not deviate significantly from the dominant corporate liberalism that was reforming the public schools underscored the problem of developing a specifically working-class education. Even Karl Marx had maintained that educational systems would always reflect the ideology of the dominant class in society. A true proletarian education could only be created by first making the proletariat the ruling class. In *Capital* Marx did argue that workers should receive a varied technical education so that they could suitably adapt to the constantly revolutionary changes in techniques as modern industry developed. While Marx's concern about technical education reflected his overall attempt to humanize the industrial process, it was certainly not a revolutionary demand nor was it only expressed by convinced Marxists.

The activities of the Pioneer Youth Clubs, which met at Manumit in the 1920s, were a more convincing form of worker's education. In this case the work of the clubs was specifically directed toward aiding the poor and the unions. During one winter the clubs investigated fire traps in Harlem, raised money and clothes for West Virginia miners, and visited textile, steel, and mining centers. But these activities did not represent a school as much as a youth movement devoted to the ideals of social reform. The work of many of the clubs was considered successful and was widely hailed by union leaders. In general the activities of the youth clubs did not replace the activities of the normal public school, but only functioned as extra-curricular activities. This was partly because of the parents who were committed to the mobility function of the schools and did not wish to remove their children from the race. Even the staff at Manumit felt it was necessary to parallel the work of the public schools so that if their pupils had to return to the regular school, they would not be behind.

During the Depression the concern about a working-class education centered around the content of the curriculum and textbooks and not around the Manumit model. In many towns throughout the country organized labor fought for control of local school boards to assure that material on labor history, the value of the union movement to society, and the closed shop were substituted for antilabor teachings. But the fight for the inclusion of these materials was not a radical departure from the goals of corporate liberalism, which defined an important role for unions in a cooperative society. In fact, the bulk of the material was not designed to create a class consciousness, but was directed toward convincing all elements of society of the value of the labor movement.

The Communist Party during the Depression also cast doubts on the possibility of a working-class education. Earl Browder, the Secretary General of the Communist Party in the United States, in 1935 expressed doubt that any program for social change could rely on the public schools to bring it about. Since 95 percent of all controlling boards in the educational system were composed of bankers and lawyers, he argued, "it is utopian to expect to change this situation fundamentally until bankers and lawyers are in general expelled from seats of power." Browder maintained that a revolutionary proletarian system of education required indoctrination into a specific form of social activity, which was impossible because of the reactionary control of education. But for Browder this did not mean that educators could do nothing. If they recognized that a class struggle existed in society, he argued, they could direct the work of the classroom toward the social and economic problems of society. The teacher could contribute to the revolutionary activities in society by breaking down the isolation between the school and everyday life. This proposal by Browder was not unique, since the cry for the involvement of the school in the life of the community had been made by progressive educators since the beginning of the century. What was different was that Browder wanted the issues placed in the framework of a class struggle instead of being used to create a sense of community and social cooperativeness.

Walden and Manumit represented the two types of alternatives that were available to the traditional common school of

America. The Walden model largely withdrew from the heavy emphasis in American education on political and social objectives. The school system, as it developed through the nineteenth and twentieth centuries was viewed primarily as a means of reforming political and social institutions, solving the problems of poverty, creating social homogeneity, developing proper social and political values, and meeting the needs of a corporate state. If all of these reasons had been eliminated from the vocabulary of educational leaders of the last two centuries, there would not have been a public school system. Many of the free schools of the 1960s followed the Walden pattern and rejected a direct concern with social reform for an emphasis on creative individual growth. This also meant a rejection of the idea of using the school as an instrument of social control. In the minds of some Americans this form of education represented a direct threat to the stability of American institutions. Many wondered if a stable society could be maintained if the proper social values were not inculcated into the child.

One of the major problems with the free school movement, one that was shared with the educational experiments in the 1920s, was that most of the students and support for these schools came from upper-middle-class and upper-class families. Experimental schools encountered a great deal of difficulty in recruiting from blue collar and lower-middle-class groups. These groups accepted the school as a mobility ladder and the proper instrument for social control. This is one reason educational radicals encountered the greatest difficulty in developing a working class form of education. As Illich claimed, most people accepted the schooling myth. While Manumit did attract workers' children in the 1920s, it did not completely disassociate itself from the public school because of anxiety about educational mobility. Unless the free school movement could find some way of directing its efforts at other social classes, their schools were in danger of becoming an elitist form of education. The most hopeful sign of developing an alternative system for the lower class was in the black community where dissatisfaction with the public school system was combined with an awareness of its traditionally discriminatory practices. But even in this case black leaders complained about the unwillingness of black parents to give up the myth of schooling. What was needed by the end of the 1960s was a new educational ideology that would provide some guidance toward truly significant alternative institutions.

chapter six
conclusion

during the twentieth century the dream of nineteenth century educational leaders was fulfilled. The school became one
of the central institutions in American society. Few Americans
were left untouched with the extension of school enrollments
in the elementary and high schools and the increased avail-
ability of institutions of higher learning. At the beginning of
the century Americans had believed the school should assume
many of the functions of what was thought to be a disintegrating community, church, and family structure. By the middle
of the century the school had extended its functions far beyond
teaching purely academic subjects and had assumed responsibility for a host of social activities ranging from driver education to providing psychological services.

But as the school expanded its activities, it also increased its
vulnerability to criticism. By becoming one of the key social
institutions it shared the burden of responsibility for many of
America's problems. The school could be viewed as a means of
combating racism and poverty, but it could also be considered
one of the central institutions contributing to continued racism
and poverty. Prejudiced teachers, segregated schools in both
the North and the South, unequal distribution of educational

monies, and the grouping of students according to ability and future vocation could all be used as examples of how the school did little more than maintain the status quo. One of the basic problems was that the school attempted to accomplish things that were beyond its power. Real changes in society depended on changes in the social structure. The opening of new areas of employment, the creation of fair employment practices, open housing legislation, and the assurance of equal poltical rights were more direct means of alleviating social problems.

On the surface it appeared by the middle of the century that Americans had come to accept the expanded and central role of the school. Newspapers each fall would report the relief of housewives as the schools reopened and resumed the care of their children after a summer of family responsibility. Parents submitted to the custodial nature of the school because it freed them from their own children. School time became everyone's time. Throughout the country family schedules were organized around the clock of the school. Vacations, alarm clocks, television programs, and family activities were all set according to school time. Even the measurement of growth changed upon entrance into the school. Before beginning school a child might have been referred to in terms of his years of growth, but after entering school he became a first or second grader. The school became so much a part of the American psyche that it was often difficult for people to recount their lives in terms other than grades through which they had passed.

Within the ranks of educators there was a continuous dialogue about the ultimate purpose of the school. The dialogue wavered between a concern about liberating the individual and providing for individual growth, and the use of the school to achieve social objectives. John Dewey had tried to wed these two objectives by couching the child's growth and freedom in terms of the individual's role within the community. Dewey's prescription failed because the school was a public institution and could not be freed from the pressures of the most powerful groups of society. Freedom and growth were compromised by attempts to instill patriotism, proper social values and manners, and by the use of the school as a source of needed labor for the economy. These social demands were the result of a variety of pressure groups working on the school. It was quite logical that since the school was of central importance in society, groups representing a variety of causes and purposes—such as the John Birch Society, the National Association for the Advancement of Colored People, the Daughters of the American Revolution, the American Civil Liberties Union, and the Students for A Democratic Society—would attempt to bring the goals of the school into line with their own objectives. School officials also represented another form of pressure group in that their personal prejudices and beliefs often set the style of the schools under their control. Pressures from society and the problems of schooling an entire society made a resolution in schools of the dialectic between freedom and social purposes impossible. During the course of the development of the school in the twentieth century the pendulum swung back and forth between the desire for a child-centered school and one designed to accomplish major social goals.

By the 1960s there appeared to be developing certain cracks in the foundation of America's faith in the school. The schools, teachers, and educational administrators traditionally had been viewed as benign and as always working in the best interests of the child. During the middle of the century this belief was brought into question not only by the actual harm the school seemed to be doing to minority groups, but also by the tremendous expense and economic waste of the school. School bond issues were defeated and some school districts in the country were forced to close their doors during part of the school year. This had occurred before under the economic pressures of the Depression, but during the 1960s these extreme economic conditions did not exist. What appeared to be happening was the realization that the school was an economic institution and could be exploited like any other economic market. The expense of education had increased with the growth of educational industries, bureaucracies, and the expansion of educational research. Publishers of tests and books and manufacturers of educational technology all developed market research skills and selling techniques designed to exploit the economic market place of the school. The consumption patterns of the school followed that of the rest of the population. The most convincingly advertised item was the most popular. Educational monies also flowed into research, which in many cases was conducted primarily because it guaranteed a position and a role to those in departments of education at major universities and colleges. For as the schools had grown in the twentieth century so also had the training grounds for teachers. The school had followed the pattern of other institutions in American society and had developed a top heavy and expensive super structure.

The general cultural revolution that started to take place in the middle of the century appeared to be directed at the centralized and manipulative role that major institutions had assumed in society. What seemed to be happening with the school, as with other institutions, was an attempt to develop a new institutional style. During the course of the twentieth century institutions had lost some of their ability to respond to the needs and desires of the people under their control. It appeared that institutions no longer existed to help people, but only existed to perpetuate themselves by controlling people. The schools had to respond in some manner to this call for change in institutional style. Decentralization, community control, the opening of new avenues of political persuasion, and the destruction of the myth of educational expertise were required if the school was to overcome its institutional paralysis. But changes of this nature required a major relocation of power. The power of control in the schools had become centralized in an educational establishment that hid behind an argument of expertise. Removing and redistributing the source of power required not only major structural changes in institutions, but also major changes in the attitudes of those in power and those governed. Progressive leaders had worked hard at the beginning of the century to create the very institutions that were being criticized by the middle of the century. The early commitment to efficiency and expertise was being partially replaced by commitment to popular democratic control. Major change depended on a reorganization of institutions or their replacement by new structures.

John Dewey often argued that history could be a trap if people failed to realize that ideas and institutions are the products of particular social conditions and problems at a particular time in history. Change could only take place if people were willing to break with history and realize that while certain ways of acting might have been suitable for the past, they were not necessarily suitable for the present. Hopefully a sense of history could lead to a more meaningful dialogue and a questioning of the nature of the existing society and its institutions.

chronological table

1914–1929: World War I to Depression

1914   Beginning of World War I
       Smith-Lever Act: federal funds for agricultural and
       home economics instruction

1916   Wilson reelected President

1917   America entered the war
       Smith-Hughes Act: began policy of promoting
       vocational education below college level through
       assistance with teachers' salaries

1918   Commission on the Reorganization of Secondary
       Education published a pamphlet, *Cardinal Principles
       of Secondary Education*
       End of war

1919   Association for the Advancement of Progressive
       Education founded. (Progressive Education Association)

1920   18th Amendment (Prohibition)
       19th Amendment (Women's Suffrage)
       Harding elected President

1921   Immigration Quota Act

1923   Death of Harding; Coolidge became President

1924   Coolidge elected President
1925   Scopes trial
1928   Hoover elected President
1929   Stock-market crash

1930–1945: Depression to End of World War II

1930   U.S. Supreme Court upheld the right of the state to
       supply textbooks to children in private, including
       parochial, schools (*Cochran* v. *Louisiana State Board
       of Education*)
1931   Japan invaded Manchuria
1932   FDR elected President
       Eight-Year Study of the Progressive Education
       Association began
1933   Hitler came to power
       Recognition of Soviet Russia
       Public Works Administration
1935   National Youth Administration: employment for college
       students
       Works Progress Administration
1936   FDR reelected
       George-Deen Act: extended the Smith-Hughes Act
1937   Japan invaded China
       Civilian Conservation Corps
1939   Outbreak of World War II
       Hitler invaded Poland
1940   FDR reelected
       Churchill Prime Minister
1941   Pearl Harbor attacked by Japan; America entered the
       war
       Lanham Act: provided federal assistance for schools in
       communities affected by the federal government's
       activities
1942   Results of Eight-Year Study published

1943 Vocational Rehabilitation Act: federal aid for disabled
     veterans
1944 FDR reelected
     The Servicemen's Readjustment Act (GI Bill): federal
     educational aid for veterans
1945 Death of FDR; Truman became President
     V-E Day: Germany surrendered
     United States dropped atomic bomb on Hiroshima
     and Nagasaki
     V-J Day: Japan surrendered
     Life adjustment education discussed in 2-day conference
     sponsored by U.S. Office of Education

1946–1973: Cold War to Cease-fire in Viet Nam

1946 George-Barden Act: extended the Smith-Hughes Act by
     increasing appropriation
     National School Lunch: gave federal funds and food to
     public and nonpublic schools; school milk program
     added 1954
1947 U.S. Supreme Court upheld a New Jersey law under
     which children in parochial schools were transported
     in regular school buses (*Everson* v. *Board of Education*)
1948 Truman elected President
1949 German Federal Republic and People's Republic of
     China established; Chinese Nationalists in Formosa
     U.S.S.R. exploded atomic bomb
1950 Korean War began
     H-bomb program initiated in the United States
     McCarthy witch-hunting campaign began
     The National Science Foundation Act—promoted
     progress in science through scholarships and
     fellowships
     Federal Impact Laws: extended the Lanham Act of
     1941; provided federal assistance to communities

affected by activities of the federal government
for construction and operation of schools

1952 Eisenhower elected President
United States exploded hydrogen bomb

1953 Truce in Korea
U.S.S.R exploded hydrogen bomb
Supreme Court clarified legal right of corporations to
make contributions to higher education

1954 *Brown* v. *Board of Education*: reversed the "separate
but equal" of *Plessy* v. *Ferguson*. Negroes were to be
admitted to white public schools
Senate censured Senator Joseph McCarthy

1955 Progressive Education Association disbanded
AFL-CIO merger

1956 Eisenhower reelected President
Civil Rights Act: first since 1875
Library Services Act: federal grants for improvement
of Library facilities

1957 Little Rock High School integrated with assistance
of armed troops
First Sputnik

1958 National Defense Education Act: provided federal
aid for education in science, mathematics, foreign
languages, counseling and guidance, educational
technology

1960 John F. Kennedy elected President

1961 Eisenhower's Farewell Address
United States broke diplomatic relations with Cuba
Bay of Pigs Invasion of Cuba
Peace Corps Act: supplied teachers and technicians
to underdeveloped nations

1962 Manpower Development and Training Act: training
for the unemployable
Government office of Science and Technology
established
James Meredith's application to University of

Mississippi denied by the Governor
Meredith began classes after U.S. Government
stepped in

1963 John Kennedy assassinated; Lyndon B. Johnson
became President
Vocational Education Act: construction of vocational
schools with expanded offerings;
extended Impact Laws and NDEA
Higher Education Facilities Act: federal grants
to all colleges, public and private, for improvement
of facilities
U.S. Supreme Court ruled that prayers and Bible
exercises in public schools and the laws requiring
them were unconstitutional (*School District of Abington
Township, Pennsylvania* v. *et al.,* v. *Schempp et al.*)

1964 Civil Rights Act: desegregation of the schools enforced
and assisted
Amendments to National Defense Education Act—
extended and expanded to include areas of English,
reading, history, and geography
Free Speech Movement at the University of California,
Berkeley
Mississippi Summer Project
LBJ elected President
Economic Opportunity Act: war on poverty through
retraining and remedial education and other
opportunities

1965 Elementary and Secondary Education Act: federal
grants to states for allocation to school districts
with low income families
National Foundation for the Arts and Humanities:
foundation to support humanities and the arts through
grants
Higher Education Act: aid to colleges, students, and
teachers
Voting Rights Act

United States began bombing North Vietnam
United States sent troops to Dominican Republic

1966 "Black Power"
1967 Nationwide urban riots
1968 Martin Luther King assassinated
Young people active in the campaign of Senator
Eugene McCarthy for Democratic nomination for
President
Robert Kennedy assassinated
Violence at Democratic National Convention in Chicago
Hubert H. Humphrey nominated by Democrats
Richard Nixon elected President
1970 U.S. invasion of Cambodia
Students shot at and killed by national guardsmen at
Kent State University (Ohio) and by policemen at
Jackson State College (Mississippi)
1972 Break-in of National Democratic Party Headquarters
at the Watergate, Washington, D.C.
Nixon reelected President
1973 Cease-fire in Viet Nam
Scandals in Nixon administration, known variously as
the Watergate Affair or the White House Horrors
Scandals investigated by Senate Committee (Ervin
Committee) and by Federal Grand Juries

_____

bibliographic note

Introduction: An Interpretive Framework

The three models of social justice are described briefly and clearly by W. G. Runciman in "The Demands of Justice," *The Listener*, July 29, 1965, pp. 152–153, 169.

The norms of social mobility were taken from Ralph G. Turner's article "Modes of Social Ascent through Education: Sponsored and Contest Mobility" in *Education, Economy, and Society: A Reader in the Sociology of Education* (New York: The Free Press, 1961), edited by A. H. Halsey, Jean Floud, and C. Arnold Anderson. The article originally appeared as "Sponsored and Contest Mobility and the School System" in the *American Sociological Review, XXV* (5), 1960.

The liberty/equality debate is covered in Herbert L. Marx, ed., *The Welfare State* (New York: H. W. Wilson, 1950) and in *The Welfare State: Menace or Millenium?* (Minnesota: Social Science Research Center of the Graduate School, 1950). Sidney Fine, *Laissez Faire and the General-Welfare State: A Study of Conflict in American Thought, 1865–1901* (Ann Arbor: University of Michigan Press, 1956) is also useful. John Stuart Mill's *On Liberty* (London: J. M. Bent and Sons, 1954) is still the classic statement on that topic. The equality theme is treated nicely by R. H. Tawney, *Equality* (London: George Allen and Unwin, 1952, 4th ed. revised). It is also covered by George L. Abernethy, ed., *The Idea of Equality: An Anthology* (Richmond, Va.: John Knox Press, 1959).

The specific relation of the ideas of liberty and equality to education is treated by Paul Nash in *Authority and Freedom in Education: An Introduction to Philosophy of Education* (New York: John Wiley and Sons, Inc., 1966). The doctrine of equality of opportunity was covered in the Winter 1968 Special Issue of *The Harvard Educational Review*. The statement of John McDermott's about the effects of the doctrine of equality of opportunity in technologically advanced societies was taken from his brilliant article, "Technology: The Opiate of the Intellectuals," a special supplement in the *New York Review of Books*, XIII (2), July 31, 1969, pp. 25–35.

Ferdinand Toennies' treatment of "Gemeinschaft and Gesellschaft" is reprinted in Volume I of *Theories of Society: Foundations of Modern Sociological Theory* (Glencoe, Ill.: The Free Press, 1961) edited by Talcott Parsons, Edward Shils, Kaspar D. Naegele, and Jesse R. Pitts. *America As a Mass Society: Changing Community and Identity* (Glencoe, Ill.: The Free Press, 1963), edited by Philip Olson, is an excellent and comprehensive treatment of many of the issues associated with community.

Chapter I: Politics, Social Justice, and the Schools

There are a number of general books that deal primarily with the twentieth century. A few of them are Frederick Lewis Allen, *The Big Change: America Transforms Itself, 1900–1950* (New York: Harper and Row, 1952); A. S. Link and William B. Catton, *American Epoch* (New York: Alfred A. Knopf, 1963); Harvey Wish, *Contemporary America* (New York: Harper and Row, 4th ed., 1966); Oscar Handlin, *The American People in the Twentieth Century* (Boston: Beacon Press, 1963); Frank

B. Freidel, *America in the Twentieth Century* (New York: Alfred A. Knopf, 1960). We drew freely from Henry Bamford Parkes and Vincent P. Carosso, *Recent America: A History, Book One: 1900–1933; Book Two: Since 1933* (New York: Thomas Y. Crowell, 1963). A book by a Frenchman, Andre Maurois, *From the New Freedom to the New Frontier: A History of the United States from 1912 to the Present* (New York: David McKay Co., Inc., 1963) translated by Patrick O'Brien, and one by an Englishman, Daniel Snowman, *USA, the Twenties to Vietnam* (London: B. T. Botsford, 1968) provide interesting perspectives of the period through foreign eyes.

A good synthesis of the decade of the 1920s can be found in John D. Hicks, *Republican Ascendancy, 1921–1933* (New York: Harper and Row, 1960). Also useful are William E. Leuchtenburg, *The Perils of Prosperity, 1914–1932* (Chicago: University of Chicago Press, 1958); Frederick L. Allen, *Only Yesterday: An informal History of the 1920's* (New York: Harper and Row, 1931); Harold V. Faulkner, *From Versailles to the New Deal* (New Haven: Yale University Press, 1951); and George Soule, *Prosperity Decade* (New York: Holt. Rinehart and Winston, 1947), the latter of which deals with the economy of the 1920s.

The most comprehensive work on the Depression and the New Deal is Arthur M. Schlesinger Jr.'s three-volume study, *The Age of Roosevelt* (Boston: Houghton Mifflin Co., 1957–1960). I. *The Crisis of the Old Order;* II. *The Coming of the New Deal;* III. *The Politics of Upheaval.* Shorter general works on the Roosevelt years include Dexter Perkins, *The New Age of Franklin D. Roosevelt, 1932–1945* (Chicago: University of Chicago Press, 1952); Frederick L. Allen, *Since Yesterday, 1929–1939,* (New York: Harper and Row, 1939); Dixon Wecter, *The Age of the Great Depression, 1929–1941* (New York: Macmillan, 1948); and Broadus Mitchell, *Depression Decade, 1929–1941* (New York: Holt, Rinehart and Winston, 1947), which is a general economic history.

A perceptive summary of the Truman and Eisenhower years is Eric F. Goldman's *The Crucial Decade—and After: America, 1945–1960,* (New York: Vintage Books, 1960). Another good general account is Herbert Agar, *The Price of Power: America Since 1945* (Chicago: University of Chicago Press, 1957), referred to in the text.

On President Kennedy there is Theodore C. Sorensen's *Kennedy* (New York: Harper and Row, 1965) and Theodore H. White's *The Making of the President 1960* (New York: Atheneum, 1961). On President Johnson's election, White's *The Making of the President, 1964* (New York: Atheneum, 1965) is quite readable.

The quote from Lord Keynes is from an essay by Robert Theobald, "Policy Formation for New Goals," in a volume edited by Theobald, *Social Policies for America in the Seventies: Nine Divergent Views* (Garden City, N.Y.: Anchor Book, 1969). Theobald's essay questions some of the assumptions of growth economists. This volume also has an article by a growth economist, Leon H. Keyserling, entitled "The Problem of Problems: Economic Growth." A sampling of Gunnar Myrdal's economic views can be found in *Challenge To Affluence* (New York: Pantheon Book, 1963) and *Beyond the Welfare State: Economic Planning and It's International Implications* (New Haven: Yale University Press, 1960).

The quote from Jack Newfield is from his *A Prophetic Minority* (New York: The New American Library, 1966), an excellent account of the radical politics of the New Left in the 1960s. The *Port Huron Statement* is reprinted in *The New Student Left*, edited by Mitchell Cohen and Dennis Hale (Boston: Beacon Press, revised ed., 1967).

A general educational history which treats in parts with the twentieth century is Henry J. Perkinson, *The Imperfect Panacea: America Faith in Education, 1865–1965* (New York: Random House, 1968). For a history of progressive education from the 1920s to the 1950s, see Lawrence A. Cremin, *The Transformation of the School* (New York: Alfred A. Knopf, 1961). Patricia A. Graham's *Progressive Education: From Arcady to Academe* (New York: Teachers College Press, 1968) is a history of the Progressive Education Association. For the tone of educational theory in the 1920s see Harold O. Rugg and Ann Shumaker, *The Child-Centered School* (Yonkers: World Book, 1928). For the 1930s see *The Educational Frontier*, edited by William H. Kilpatrick (New York: The Century Co., 1933). For a detailed analysis of progressive education in the 1930s see C. A. Bowers, *The Progressive Educator and the Depression —The Radical Years* (New York: Random House, 1969).

Examples of the criticism of public schools and of progressive education in the 1950s are Arthur E. Bestor's *Educational Wastelands* (Urbana, Ill.: University of Illinois Press, 1953) and Albert Lynd's *Quackery in the Public Schools* (Boston: Little and Co., 1953). Mary Ann Raywid in *The Ax-Grinders* (New York: The Macmillan Company, 1962) treated with criticisms of the public schools, particularly with the Council for Basic Education. Admiral Rickover's educational proposals are in his *Education and Freedom* (New York: Dutton, 1959).

Jerome Bruner's *The Process of Education* (Cambridge: Harvard University Press, 1960) reflects the cognitive emphasis of the 1960s.

Chapter II: War, Machines, and Education

President Eisenhower's Farewell Address can be found in *Public Papers of the Presidents*. Senator Fulbright's speech can be found in the *Congressional Record* of December 13, 1967.

The phrase an "age of total war" was adapted from Arthur Marwick's *Britain in the Century of Total War: War, Peace and Social Change, 1900–1967* (London: Bodley Head, 1968). For America's involvement in World War I see Charles Seymour, *Woodrow Wilson and the World War* (New Haven: Yale University Press, 1921); Frederic L. Paxon, *America at War, 1917–1918* (Boston: Houghton Mifflin Company, 1939); and Pierce G. Fredericks, *The Great Adventure: America in the First World War* (New York: E. P. Dutton and Co., 1960). For World War II see Louis L. Snyder, *The War: A Concise History,*

1939–1945 (New York: Julian Messner, 1960); and Fletcher Pratt, *War for the World* (New Haven: Yale University Press, 1951). Eliot Janeway's *The Struggle for Survival* (New Haven: Yale University Press, 1951) is the story of the war at home. For a critical analysis of the received truth about the politics of World War II see Gabriel Kolko, *The Politics of War* (New York: Random House, 1969).

For America's foreign policy in the twentieth century see R. Leopold, *Growth of American Foreign Policy* (New York: Alfred A. Knopf, 1962); and William A. Williams, *The Tragedy of American Diplomacy* (Cleveland: World Publishing Company, 1959). George Kennan's containment article is in a collection of his essays, *American Diplomacy, 1900–1950* (Chicago: University of Chicago Press, 1951). America's foreign policy since 1945 is covered by John W. Spanier, *American Foreign Policy Since World War Two* (New York: Praeger, 1965). A book that shows America's conservative role in foreign affairs is David Horowitz's *Empire and Revolution: A Radical Interpretation of Contemporary History* (New York: Random House, 1969).

The quote from the Air Force Association is from Volume III of *The Autobiography of Bertrand Russell* (London: George Allen and Unwin Ltd., 1969).

The phrase "the warfare state" is from Fred J. Cook's *The Warfare State* (New York: Macmillan, 1962). The extent and the effects of the warfare state are studied in two books by Seymour Melman: *Our Depleted Society* (New York: Holt, Rinehart and Winston, 1965); and *Pentagon Capitalism: The Political Economy of War* (New York: McGraw-Hill, 1970).

Pragmatism is covered by Edward C. Moore, *American Pragmatism* (New York: Columbia University Press, 1961); Philip P. Wiener, *Evolution and the Founders of Pragmatism* (Cambridge: Harvard University Press, 1949); and by Morton White, ed., *The Age of Analysis: 20th Century Philosophers* (New York: The New American Library, 1955). A few of Dewey's own works should be consulted, for example, *Democracy and Education*

(New York: Macmillan, 1916); *How We Think* (New York: Holt, 1922); and *The School and Society* (Chicago: University of Chicago Press, 1899). For an analysis and criticism of Dewey's pragmatic liberalism see Edgar B. Gumbert, "John Dewey and the New Liberalism: Reactions to the U.S.S.R.," *Educational Theory, XXII* (3), Summer 1972, pp. 344–359.

A short study of the interplay between community and corporation and the effects they have had on each other is W. Lloyd Warner's *The Corporation in the Emergent American Society* (New York: Harper, 1962). Philip Olson (op. cit.) is also helpful.

Max Weber's study of types of authority is reprinted in Parson, Shils, Naegele, and Pitts (op. cit.).

In addition to William H. Whyte's *The Organization Man* (New York: Simon and Schuster, 1956), mentioned in the text, other outstanding books of the 1950s treating class and power and changes in American life and character were C. Wright Mills' two works, *White Collar* (New York: Oxford University Press, 1951) and *The Power Elite* (New York: Oxford University Press, 1956); and David Riesman's *The Lonely Crowd* (New Haven: Yale University Press, 1950).

The quote from John Holt about feeling unfree is from his essay in the book edited by Robert Theobold, already cited. The quote from Paul Goodman about Dewey is from *Compulsory Mis-Education and Community of Scholars* (New York: Vintage, 1964). The quotes from Charles W. Eliot and from Jane Addams are from *The Public Life, I* (15), August 8, 1969, p. 3. The quote from James A. Perkins about interlocking elites is from a commencement address he gave to the University of Notre Dame, reprinted in part in *The Chronicle of Higher Education, II* (19), June 10, 1968, p. 4.

For the development of higher education see in addition to Kerr's work cited in the text Laurence R. Veysey, *The Emergence of the American University* (Chicago: University of Chicago Press, 1965); Frederick Rudolph, *American College and University* (New York: Alfred A. Knopf, 1962); and Christopher

Jencks and David Riesman, *The Academic Revolution* (Garden City, N.Y.: Doubleday, 1968).

For the antiintellectualism and the social control aspects of progressive intellectuals, including Dewey, see Christopher Lasch, *The New Radicalism in America: 1889–1963. The Intellectual as a Social Type* (New York: Alfred A. Knopf, 1965). For the way an intellectual elite has come to hold power in the United States see Noam Chomsky, *American Power and the New Mandarins* (New York: Pantheon Books, 1969). An analysis of a youthful counter culture is Theodore Roszak's *The Making of a Counter Culture: Reflections on the Technocratic Society and Its Youthful Opposition* (Garden City, N.Y.: Anchor Books, 1969).

Chapter III: Intelligence Testing and the Efficient Society

Historians have given increasing attention to the influence of concepts of efficiency in the development of the modern school. Edward Krug's *The Shaping of the American High School* (New York: Harper & Row, 1964) traces the development of the idea of social efficiency among educators at the beginning of the century and the impact the concept had on the development of the modern high school. Krug's book has an extensive bibliography and is rich in detail. If one is interested in pursuing the study of this concept, it would be worthwhile to begin with this work. Another helpful book is Walter Drost's biography, *David Snedden and Education for Social Efficiency* (Madison: University of Wisconsin Press, 1967). Raymond Callahan's *Education and the Cult of Efficiency* (Chicago: University of Chicago Press, 1962) is an excellent study of the influence of business concepts of efficiency on the development of school administration. The best way of capturing the flavor of the efficiency rhetoric is to go directly to the sources. One might begin with Henry Herbert Goddard's *Human Efficiency and Levels of Intelligence* (Princeton: Princeton University Press, 1920). Goddard is interesting and important because of his work in the intelligence movement and his pioneering work in special education. One of the finest statements of the efficiency ideology by one of the leading educators of the twentieth century is Edward L. Thorndike's *Human Nature and the Social Order* (New York: Macmillan Co., 1940).

One of the best summaries of past and present trends in work on intelligence is Arthur Jensen's "How Much Can We Boost I.Q. and Scholastic Achievement" in the Winter 1969 issue of *Harvard Educational Review*. This article is important not only as a resource item, but also because of the controversy it caused at the time of publication. Jensen is representative of the presently unpopular belief in native intelligence. For an understanding of the development of intelligence testing and concepts of intelligence, it is advisable to begin with Alfred Binet and Theodore Simon's *The Development of Intelligence in Children* (Baltimore: Williams and Wilkins Co., 1916). Henry Herbert Goddard's *Feeble-Mindedness: Its Causes and Consequences* (New York: The Macmillan Company, 1914) provides some interesting and influential views about the relationship of levels of intelligence to social problems. The story of the development of the Alpha and Beta tests can be found in "Psychological Examining in the United States Army," edited by Robert M. Yerkes in Volume 15 of the *National Academy of Sciences Memoirs* (Washington Government Printing Office 1921) and in *Army Mental Tests*, compiled and edited by Clarence S. Yoakum and Robert M. Yerkes (New York: Henry Holt and Company, 1920). The racial interpretations of the early intelligence tests can be found in Carl C. Brigham's *A Study of American Intelligence* (Princeton: Princeton University Press, 1923). The major debates on the meaning of intelligence can be found in "Intelligence and its Measurement: A Symposium," *The Journal of Educational Psychology*, Vol. XII. The debate begins in the March 1921 issue and continues through the year. The best sources for the continuing debate about the meaning of intelligence and its relationship to nature and nurture are the 1928 and 1940 yearbooks of the National Society for the Study of

Education. The 1928 yearbook was titled *Nature and Nurture* (Bloomington: Public School Publishing House, 1928) and the 1940 yearbook was titled *Intelligence: Its Nature and Nurture* (Bloomington: Public School Publishing House, 1940).

Criticisms of the efficiency concept of schooling and society have come from many different perspectives. One important source for reaction against the idea of native intelligence are the rebuttals to Arthur Jensen's article in the Summer 1969 issue of the *Harvard Educational Review*. Sociological studies have tended to show that the efficiency concept of schooling has led to the use of the school as a means of cementing existing social classes. Two classic studies in this area are August Hollingshead's *Elmstown's Youth* (New York: J. Wiley, 1949) and Patricia Sexton's *Education and Income* (New York: Viking Press, 1961). Michael Young's *The Rise of the Meritocracy* (London: Thames & Hudson, 1958) is an important satire of the possible results of selectivity in the schools on English society. A popular and important criticism is Kurt Vonnegut's *Player Piano* (New York: Scribner, 1952). This book highlights the problems of an efficiency oriented society with the style of a good novelist.

Chapter IV: Youth and the Custodial Role of the Schools

The attitude that children and youth were being displaced from modern social structure was reflected by many writers at the beginning of the twentieth century. One of the most important statements was John Dewey's *School and Society* (Chicago: University of Chicago, 1899). This same feeling was reflected in an autobiographical fashion by educator Caroline Pratt in *I Learn from Children* (New York: Simon & Schuster, 1948). G. Stanley Hall's *Adolescence* (New York: D. Appleton and Company, 1904) represents the beginning of the modern concept of adolescence and a concern about its role in the modern urban and industrial world. Another important collection of Hall's writings can be found in *Health, Growth and Heredity:*

G. Stanley Hall on Natural Education (New York: Teachers College, 1965) edited by Charles Burgess and Charles Strickland. One of the clearest statements of social control ideology with regard to the modern world and the education of the child is Edward Ross's *Social Control* (New York: The MacMillan Co., 1904). For a criticism of the social purposes of schooling see Edgar B. Gumbert, "A Proposal for Copping Out," *The Educational Forum*, November 1971, pp. 47–54.

One of the earliest sources for attitudes about education in an urban environment can be found in William Oland Bourne's *History of the Public School Society of the City of New York* (New York: Wm. Woodland Co., 1870). The best sources for understanding the attitudes toward the problems of children and the city in the 1890s are Jacob Riis's *Children of the Tenements* (New York: Macmillan, 1903) and *How the Other Half Lives* (New York: C. Scribner, 1890). The story of the playground movement is told in Henry Curtis's *The Play Movement and its Significance* (New York: MacMillan, 1917).

Early twentieth century attitudes toward juvenile gangs can be found in J. Addams Puffer *The Boy and His Gang* (Boston: Houghton Mifflin & Co., 1912) and Fredric Thrasher's *The Gang* (Chicago: University of Chicago Press, 1927). The sociological work of the Chicago School of Urban Studies is summarized in Robert Park's *The City* (Chicago: University of Chicago Press, 1928). A more recent work dealing with the problem of youth and the cities is James Bryant Conant's *Slums and Suburbs* (New York: McGraw-Hill, 1961). For suggestions on how to use the city for educational purposes see Edgar B. Gumbert, "The City as Educator," *Education and Urban Society*, IV (1) November 1971, pp. 7–24.

The best source of information on changes in school enrollment, productivity rates, population changes, and economic growth in the United States is *Long Term Economic Growth 1860–1965* (Washington: Superintendent of Documents, 1966) issued by the Bureau of the Census of the United States Department of Commerce. This volume should be a standard resource item for those interested in the development of the United States in both economic and cultural terms. Changes in population distribution between rural and urban, changes in school attendance, and the age distribution of the labor force in different types of occupations tell a great deal about the development of the United States.

The appearance of the generation gap during the 1920s was reflected throughout the literature of the world. The best place to begin is *Literary Digest*'s national survey of attitudes toward the younger generation. This can be found in "Case Against the Younger Generation," *Literary Digest* (June 17, 1922). Examples of discussions about automobiles and morality can be found in the August 1, 1925 and October 1, 1925 issues of *Survey*. A discussion of the new morality of youth can be found in two statements by college girls titled "Has Youth Deteriorated?" in the July 1926 issue of *Forum*. W. H. Cowley's "Explaining the Rah Rah Boy" in the *New Republic* (April 14, 1926) is a statement of concern and description of the college student of the 1920s. The article "The League of Youth" in the *New Republic* (June 28, 1922) expresses the hope that the rah-rah spirit of college youth can be directed to more important social concerns.

The problems of youth during the depression years are summarized by Harold Rugg in *Foundations for American Education* (New York: World Book Company, 1947). A survey of youth's attitudes during the Depression can be found in Howard M. Bell's *Youth Tell Their Story* (Washington: The American Council on Education, 1938). Other studies by the American Youth Commission are important sources for this period. They include the general report of the commission titled *Youth and the Future* (Washington: The American Council on Education, 1942) Lewis L. Lorwin's *Youth Work Programs* (Washington: The American Council on Education, 1941); and M. M. Chambers's *Youth-Serving Organizations* (Washington: The American Council on Education, 1937).

The discussion of the problems of getting youth back into

school after World War II can be found in N. B. Henry's "Shifting Problems of Youth Employment," *School Review* (January 1967); H. A. Anderson's "Youth Work and the Schools," *School Review* (September 1947); and E. A. Merritt and H. S. Rifkind's "Unemployment among the Teen-aged in 1947–49," *Monthly Labor Review* (December 1949).

The early definition of the beat generation is in an article by Cellon Holmes titled "This is the Beat Generation" in the November 16, 1952 issue of the *New York Times Magazine*. Jack Kerouac's novels *On the Road* (New York: Viking Press, 1957) and *The Darhma Bums* (New York: Viking Press, 1958) represent the classic statements of beat literature. The story of the transition from the beat culture of the 1950s to the counter culture of the 1960s is told in an autobiographical fashion by Abbie Hoffman in *Woodstock Nation* (New York: Vintage Books, 1969) and by Jerry Rubin in *Do It!* (New York: Simon and Schuster, 1970). These two books are important not only because of their autobiographical style but also as statements of the youth culture of the 1960s. One interesting study of the ideology of the youth culture of the 1960s is Theodore Roszak's *The Making of a Counter Culture* (New York: Anchor Books, 1968). Radical youth were influenced by the thought of Herbert Marcuse; see, for example, his *Eros And Civilization: A Philosophical Inquiry Into Freud* (New York: Vintage Books, 1962) and *One-Dimensional Man* (Boston: Beacon Press, 1964).

Chapter V: The Search for Alternatives

The most critical statements about the existence of the school can be found in Ivan D. Illich's collection of essays entitled *Celebration of Awareness: A Call for Institutional Revolution* (Garden City, N. Y.: Doubleday & Company, Inc., 1970) and in his *Deschooling Society* (New York: Harper and Row, 1971). For related statements see Everett Reimer's *School is Dead: Alternatives in Education* (Garden City, N.Y.: Doubleday and Co., Inc., 1971).

An historical context for the search for alternatives can be found in Joel H. Spring's *Education and the Rise of the Corporate State* (Boston: Beacon Press, 1972) and in *Roots of Crisis: American Education in the Twentieth Century* (Chicago: Rand McNally and Co., 1973) by Clarence Karier, Paul C. Violas, and Joel Spring.

Paul Goodman's concern about the effects of the school and the alienation of youth is expressed in *Growing Up Absurd* (New York: Vintage, 1956) and in *Compulsory Miseducation* (New York: Vintage, 1962). Edgar Friedenberg's early classic on adolescence is titled *The Vanishing Adolescent* (New York: Dell, 1959) and his major work on the relationship of the school to adolescent growth is *Coming of Age in America* (New York: Vintage, 1963).

The 1960s witnessed the growth of a whole body of educational and psychological literature that was to be associated with the "free school" movement. George Leonard's *Education and Ecstasy* (New York: Dell, 1968) represented an utopian hope of combining sensitivity training with the new educational technology. Jonathan Kozol's *Death at an Early Age* (New York: Houghton Mifflin Co., 1967) was an indictment against the Boston public schools for destroying the hearts and minds of Negro children. A. S. Neill's *Summerhill: A Radical Approach to Child Rearing* (New York: Hart Publishing Co., 1960) became one of the models for many of the new schools. John Holt's *How Children Learn* (New York: Pitman, 1967) and *How Children Fail* (New York: Pitman Publishing Corp., 1964) provided newer approaches to understanding the effect of the classroom and teaching style on the learning of the child. Also popular reading in this field were James Herndon's *The Way it Spozed to Be* (New York: Simon and Schuster, 1965) and Neil Postman and C. Weingartner's *Teaching as a Subversive Activity* (New York: Delacorte Press, 1969). Among the popular psychological literature of the "free school" movement was Rollo May's *Man's Search for Himself* (New York: Signet, 1967); Carl Rogers' *On Becoming A Person* (New

York: Houghton Hifflin and Co., 1961); R. D. Laing's *The Politics of Experience* (New York: Pantheon Books, 1967); and Erich Fromm's *The Art of Loving* (New York: Harper, 1956). Radical approaches to instruction were suggested by Paulo Friere in *Pedagogy of the Oppressed* (New York: Herder and Herder, 1970).

Information about how to start a "free school" and an attempt to appraise the movement can be found in the *Raspberry Greenways' Exercises: How to Start Your Own School—and Make a Book* (Freestone, California: The Freestone Press, 1970). *This Magazine Is About Schools* contains many articles on the new school movement. Several centers for distribution of information about the new school movement existed. One of the most active was the New Schools Exchange in Santa Barbara, California. Another center that concentrated on placing teachers in the new schools was the Teacher Drop-Out Center in Amherst Massachusetts. Issues of the *New York Review of Books* contain many informative articles. For a criticism of the free school movement see Jonathan Kozol's *Free Schools* (New York: Houghton Mifflin Co., 1973).

Several books cover various aspects of the new schools of the Twenties. One major source of general information is Harold Rugg and Ann Shumaker's *The Child-Centered School* (Yonkers-on-the-Hudson, New York: World Book Co., 1928). Another source of general information is Agnes De Lima's *Our Enemy the Child* (New York: New Republic, Inc., 1926). Margaret Naumberg's major work on education is the *Child and the World* (New York: Harcourt, Brace and Co., 1928). Of particular importance for understanding Naumberg's attitude toward Dewey is her article in the September 15, 1928 issue of *Survey* titled "A Challenge to John Dewey" and one in the June 25th, 1930 issue of *The New Republic* titled "The Crux of Progressive Education." Information about Manumit School can be found in Nellie M. Seeds' "Democracy in the Making at Manumit School," *Nation* (June 1927); Devere Allen's "A School for Workers' Children," *Nation* (October 1924); and William Mann

Finck's "An Adventure in Extending the Horizons of Children," *Progressive Education* (November 1937). The best statement on communism and education in the 1930s is Earl Browder's "Education—an Ally in the Workers' Struggle," *The Social Frontier* (January 1935).

name and title index

subject index